Eva Wong's research on the Malaysian Asser[illegible] God breaks ground in two ways: as the first academic study of the denomination's history and by employing Joel's passage as the interpretive tool. This creative study may serve as a model for constructing Pentecostal histories, particularly from the global South.

Wonsuk Ma, PhD, Dean, Distinguished Professor of Global Christianity, College of Theology and Ministry at Oral Roberts University, Tulsa, OK, USA

I am delighted with this book which traces the history of the Pentecostal movement in Malaysia and imparts phenomenological incidence of dramatic revival meetings, which is a thrill to me. It is accurate to say that Pentecostal revivalism involves ongoing spiritual regeneration in order to rekindle the desire to carry out missions and engage in evangelism. An enriching part is the analysis of the Pentecostal theological component. The importance of modern Pentecostal spirituality in today's Pentecostalism in Malaysia and around the world cannot be overstated in terms of preserving Pentecostal individuality. It excites and challenges the entire world's religious community, not just the Pentecostal Church.

Julie Ma, PhD, Professor of Intercultural Studies and Mission at Oral Roberts University, Tulsa, OK, USA

Eva Wong's study of the shift of the Assemblies of God of Malaysia from being a classical Pentecostal movement to a contemporary Pentecostal church movement highlights a phenomenon which is replicated in many other places. Wong's affirmative yet critical assessment should serve as a serious warning to those who are too eager to join the charismatic bandwagon of the Third Wave. At the same time, her judicious recommendations suggest that the future is hopeful.

Revd Dr Simon Chan was formerly Earnest Lau Professor of Systematic Theology at Trinity Theological College, Singapore, and currently editor of Asia Journal of Theology

Here is an insightful book which takes readers on a theological as well as a practical journey of the Pentecostal movement in the context of Malaysia. Dr Wong has written a must-read textbook for Pentecostal studies, which analytically explains how the classical understanding of Pentecostalism has been contextualised in a South Asian country where Islam is the dominant religion. Theological considerations and practical suggestions for re-orienting Pentecostalism in Malaysia based on the extensive research results are also invaluable contributions that this book brings to readers in the region as well as to Pentecostal audiences worldwide.

Revd Dr Guichun Jun, Yoido Pentecostal Research Tutor, Oxford Centre for Mission Studies Admission Tutor, and Book Review Editor of Transformation

The Day of the Lord in Malaysia

About the Author

Eva Wong (PhD, Oxford Centre for Mission Studies in partnership with Middlesex University) is a full-time faculty of the Bible College of Malaysia, an Assemblies of God minister, and the Director of Malaysia Pentecostal Research Centre. She currently serves in the Assemblies of God Theological Commission, the Executive Committee of the Asia Pentecostal Society, and the Lausanne Global Analysis Editorial Advisory Board.

The Day of the Lord in Malaysia

Classical to Contemporary Pentecostalism in the Assemblies of God with reference to Joel 2:28-32

Eva Wong Suk Kyun

regnum

First published 2023 by Regnum Books International

This book is an abridged version of Eva Wong Suk Kyun's thesis, "Contextual Pentecostalism from a Classical Pentecostal Movement to a Contemporary Pentecostal Church Movement: A Study of the Assemblies of God of Malaysia with Special Reference to Joel 2:28-32"

Regnum is an imprint of the Oxford Centre for Mission Studies
St. Philip and St. James Church
Woodstock Road, Oxford OX2 6HR, UK
www.regnumbooks.net

British Library Cataloguing in Publication Data. A catalogue record for this book is available from the British Library.

ISBN: 979-8-8898-3311-6
eBook ISBN: 979-8-8898-3312-3

Typeset in Candara by Words by Design.

Photo by Glitch Lab App, unsplash.com

The publication of this volume is made possible through the financial assistance of Evangelisches Missionswerk.

Distributed by Fortress Press in the US, Canada, India, and Brazil

Dedication

I dedicate this book to my inspirational and benevolent mentors: Revd Drs Wonsuk and Julie Ma, and Revd Dr Simon Chan.

Contents

Acknowledgements

My heart is full of praise and thanksgiving to God for His lovingkindness, providence, and blessings upon my life, and for His strength and abundant grace that enabled me to complete this research journey. I am truly blessed by the great support of many parties and noble individuals who have made this thesis possible. Special thanks to Drs Paul and Liz Bendor-Samuel, Revd Drs Wonsuk and Julie Ma, Dr David Cranston, Dr Thomas Harvey, Dr David Singh, Revd Dr Simon Chan, Revd Dr Guichun Jun, Dr Joyce Every-Clayton, Revd Ng Kok Kee, Revd Dr Victor Lee, OCMS, SLI, EMW, AGM, and BCM.

Gratitude to my loving parents, Andrew and Grace Wong, my husband, Philip Chong, my daughter, Clarissa, and son, Trevor, who always pray for me, and whom I love deeply: thank you. They have loved and supported me so selflessly for many years in this research journey that much of our precious time has been sown into this long-haul study, and I am forever grateful to God for all His blessings and providence through the many individuals and my loving family.

This book is based on a Middlesex University PhD thesis done at the Oxford Centre for Mission Studies and the full details of the research methods can be found in the thesis.[1]

List of Abbreviations

AG – Assemblies of God
AGM – Assemblies of God of Malaysia
AGMS – Assemblies of God of Malaya and Singapore
AGUSA – Assemblies of God, United States of America
BCM – Bible College of Malaysia

[1] ESK Wong, 'Contextual Pentecostalism from a Classical Pentecostal Movement to a Contemporary Pentecostal Church Movement: A Study of the Assemblies of God of Malaysia with Special Reference to Joel 2:28-32' (PhD thesis, Middlesex University, UK, 2022).

Chapter One
Contextual Malaysian Pentecostal Spirituality

The globalisation of Pentecostalism over the past century and its ongoing rapid growth from 981,000 adherents in 1900 to 635 million adherents in 2020, from all Spirit-filled renewals worldwide, has been phenomenal. 86% of all Pentecostals and Charismatics are in the Global South and this represents the fastest-growing Christian group worldwide in the twenty-first century. The prophecy of Joel 2:28-32 and its fulfilment on the Day of Pentecost in Acts 2 have featured prominently as being the foundational scripture to classical Pentecostal theology, and the Pentecostal faith has gradually adapted to the changes in the local sociopolitical, economic, religious, and cultural landscape.

The main theme of this research was to understand the changing nature of the Assemblies of God of Malaysia (AGM) over six decades, from classical to contemporary, in the Malaysian sociocultural and religious context, and to question whether the changes are evolutions, valid enculturation, or drifts which create an increasing gap and tension between the espoused Pentecostal theology and its practice.

In the last decade, there has been a strong focus on prayer for revival and there have also been changes in the nature and concept of the Voice of the Spirit in contemporary practices.

Outpouring of the Spirit in Joel's Prophecy (2:28-32) and Acts 2:16-21

The outpouring of the Spirit is associated with Spirit-baptism.[2] Joel's prophecy in 2:28-32 signifies God pouring out the 'Holy Spirit' in Spirit-baptism in a new and powerful way, as affirmed by Peter on the Day of Pentecost (Acts 2:17-21; 2:1-2). The fulfilment of Joel 2 in Acts 2 is affirmed by many New Testament scholars, and the present-day revival and outpouring of the Spirit shows its centrality and theological importance as the foundational scripture in the classical Pentecostal theology and Pentecostalism. This remains a strong emphasis in the movement today.

Baptism in the Holy Spirit is 'the crown jewel of Pentecostal distinctives' as defined by Frank Macchia. It is the central doctrine from which all the other interrelated theological themes can be analysed. According to Simon Chan and Macchia, Baptism in the Holy Spirit is understood as a theophanic experience of being filled with the presence of God, a spiritual encounter and relationship with the triune God. The spiritual dimensions and roles of glossolalia in Christian spirituality are much broader than just 'initial evidence' of Baptism in the Holy Spirit. There is a need to develop coherent theological explanations for these central doctrines of Pentecostal distinctives.

---

[2] The terms 'Baptism in the Holy Spirit' and 'Spirit-baptism' are used interchangeably in this research.

The outpouring of the Spirit on 'all flesh' means Baptism in the Holy Spirit is a gift to all peoples, transcending age, marital status, gender, and social status, and that everyone can receive Baptism in the Holy Spirit and spiritual gifts, especially the nine gifts in 1 Corinthians 12:8-10, and empowerment for life and service. Classical Pentecostals understand Baptism in the Holy Spirit as a prophetic community empowered for missions, and many early Pentecostal women missionaries have been sent out and have served in leadership roles as pioneers, preachers, educators, ministers, and missionaries worldwide.

As Acts refers to Baptism in the Holy Spirit as occurring 'in the last days', early Pentecostals from the Azusa Street revival understood the 'last days' as meaning that they were living in the days of the imminent return of Christ. Their belief in the apocalyptic vision of the 'last days' spurred the eschatological fervour and missionary emphasis for worldwide evangelism before Christ's return. The universal missionary endeavour led to the globalisation of the Pentecostal movement in the following decades. Over time, the 'crisis' eschatology faded as some modern Pentecostals begin to understand 'last days' in terms of salvation history.

Prayer for Revival

In recent years, there has been a strong prayer movement for revival. Early Pentecostals understood revival as a new pouring of the Spirit in fulfilment of Joel 2–Acts 2. The first issue of *The Apostolic Faith* newsletter during the Azusa Street revival in 1906 reported in the headlines 'Pentecost Has Come: Los Angeles Being Visited by a Revival of Bible Salvation and Pentecost as Recorded in the Book of

Acts.' There is a deep desire within the AGM for a mighty outpouring of the Holy Spirit once again, a yearning for another wave of revival, as well as dependency upon the leading of the Holy Spirit through the Voice of the Spirit and the Spirit's empowerment for the spread of the gospel.

The current prayer movement and focus on revival reflect a strong theological understanding and spiritual conviction of the essence of Pentecostalism being the outpouring of the Spirit as prophesied by Joel and its fulfilment on the Day of Pentecost, and ongoing fulfilment in the church era. The AGM uses the passage in Joel 2 to call for solemn assemblies, prayer and fasting, repentance and intercession before God on behalf of the land, seeking God that He would relent judgment upon the nation and pour out his Spirit and 'heal our land'.

Voice of the Spirit

Joel prophesied that with the coming of the Spirit there will be prophecies, dreams, and visions. I will use the Pentecostal parlance 'Voice of the Spirit' as shorthand for the Spirit's speaking through prophecies, dreams, and visions.

Pentecostals did and perhaps still do believe that prophecies, dreams, and visions are significant in confirming one's calling to the ministry; hence, there is a need to study the significance of the Voice of the Spirit in the calling of full-time ministers from the pioneering period to present.

The Voice of the Spirit is the Holy Spirit's guidance, often expressed as 'being led by the Spirit', and it plays a major role in the AGM's missiology, ecclesiology, and ministerial aspects, and in the growth of the AGM through the six decades.

The AGM as a classical Pentecostal movement is rooted in the prophecy of Joel 2:28-32 (and Acts 2:16-21), but there has been a fundamental change of image, outlook, and practices through the different historical periods. These changes are reflected in the AGM's shift of self-designation from being a classical Pentecostal movement to a contemporary Pentecostal Church movement in 2018, and they affect its theology and ministerial perspectives as it embarks on new strategies and developments in the twenty-first century.

The AGM was established by missionaries from the Assemblies of God of USA (AGUSA) and inherited the classical Pentecostal theology and the USA's Tenets of Faith. Their new image, 'A Contemporary Pentecostal Church Movement', was first discussed by the Executive Committee in 2015. Its vision comprises winning the lost, making disciples, church planting, social concern, reaching all nations, having healthy, Spirit-filled churches with strong leadership, Pentecostal fervour, nurturing the young generation, and having excellent facilities to serve the community.

Pentecostal Distinctives and Revivalism

Baptism in the Holy Spirit, glossolalia, and missions are the main Pentecostal distinctives stated in the AG's Tenets of Faith, and the Voice of the Spirit is an implicit theology and practice shaped by Joel's prophecy.

The AG believe that the experience of Baptism in the Holy Spirit is a distinct and subsequent experience of salvation or born again, as was the normal experience in the early Christian church (Acts 8:12-27; 10:44-46; 11:14-16; 15:7-9) with the initial physical evidence of speaking in tongues (Acts 2:4), and the empowerment for missions (Acts 1:8). This Pentecostal view differs from the typical evangelical teachings that Baptism in the Holy Spirit happens during conversion when a person accepts Jesus Christ as Saviour. Most Charismatics (1960s–1970s) also believe in Baptism in the Holy Spirit as subsequent to conversion but not necessarily with speaking in tongues as evidence. Third Wavers or Neo-Charismatics (1980s onward) emphasise signs and wonders and spiritual gifts, but do not believe in Baptism in the Holy Spirit as the second work of grace subsequent to conversion, and speaking in tongues is not necessary.

The term 'latter rain' was used in the doctrine of the early Pentecostal belief in the 1900s, derived from early hermeneutics on the 'lost and restored' imagery in Joel 2–Acts 2 and the fulfilment of the 'Latter Rain' covenant (Joel 2:23 and James 5:7). Early Pentecostals believed it was the restoration of the apostolic faith with the ninefold gifts of the Spirit in the last days, with the urgency to save souls. This was different from the controversial 'Latter Rain Movement' or 'New Order of the Latter Rain', which emerged in the 1940s and became one of the catalysts for the Charismatic movements in the 1960s and 1970s, and the restoration of the fivefold ministries. Today, Pentecostals refer to the 'latter rain' as revival or God pouring out his Spirit.

The early Pentecostals from the Azusa Street revival understood the eschatological theme 'in the last days' meant they were living in the days of the imminent return of Christ. The AGM's espoused theology and founding experience were heavily influenced by this apocalyptic vision. However, dispensationalism has waned in the second half of the twentieth century as the classical Pentecostals in the 1980s joined the evangelical family, who understand the 'last days' in Acts 2 as the period from the Incarnation of Jesus Christ to Parousia.

The early and classical Pentecostals understood revival as the outpouring of the Holy Spirit on the Day of Pentecost and continuous fulfilment of Joel's prophecy in the church era, like the Azusa Street revival and thereafter. Pentecostal revivalism is a continuous spiritual renewal in restoring the passion to engage in evangelism and missions. From the 1990s to contemporary times, there has been a global revival movement, particularly from the influences of John Wimber (1934–1997) and Peter C. Wagner (1930–2016) of the Third Wave, which spurred much revivalism among Malaysian Pentecostal and Charismatic churches through international networks. Their revivalist spirituality emphasises spiritual warfare, demonology, signs and wonders, and apostolic and prophetic movement.

The AGM's Origin

Although the AGUSA started missionary work in Malaya in the 1930s, 1957 was the year of the official formation of the General Council. From the 1930s to 1960s – a foreign missionary period – everything was sent from the USA, Hong Kong, and Singapore. In general, it can be said that the AGM's doctrine and teaching during the first 40 years from 1957 closely followed the Pentecostal teaching received from the pioneering American missionaries. The AGM's teaching on espoused classical Pentecostal theology in the first four decades was also similar to, if not identical with, the AG missionaries.

The AGM in a Malaysian Context

Malaysia is a multiracial, multicultural, and multireligious country. At the time of writing (2020), the current Malaysian population is around 32 million. Malaysia's ethnicity comprises 69% Malay and indigenous, 23% Chinese, 7% Indian, and 1% other. The religious demography is 64% Muslim, 18% Buddhist, 9% Christian (the majority in East Malaysia), and 6% Hindu. Pentecostals represent 14% of Christianity in Malaysia, Evangelicals 17% and Roman Catholics 54%.

The AGM is a member of the National Evangelical Christian Fellowship, one of the three component bodies of the Christian Federation of Malaysia, along with the Council of Churches of Malaysia and the Catholic Bishops' Conference of Malaysia. AGM churches claimed 49,810 adherents in 2020: 2% of the Christian population.

Islam has been the national religion since Malayan independence in 1957. Although there is 'freedom of religion', there are many restrictions that have shaped Christian mission in the country. Propagating religious faith to a Muslim is prohibited by law, and there has been an increasing Islamic resurgence and Islamisation since 1970.

The Early Missionary Period

Malaysian Pentecostalism owes its shape to the early missionary period before the 1950s, paving the way to a unique spirituality. Missionaries from the mainline traditional Christian denominations had arrived in Malaya (now West Malaysia) and Borneo (East

Malaysia) much earlier than the Pentecostals. Historians suggest that Nestorian missionaries from Syria had travelled through the Silk Road to the Malay Archipelago as early as the seventh century in the north-west of the Malay Peninsula and North Sumatra. Since the sixteenth century, the rule of Portuguese (1511), Dutch (1641), and British (1786) opened doors to Roman Catholicism (1511) and Protestantism. Christianity grew during the British rule in the nineteenth century, when missionary work began in the Straits Settlements and Borneo. Pentecostal missionaries only came to Malaya in the twentieth century from the AGUSA, along with other streams mainly from Ceylon, China, Finland, and Hong Kong. The Australian missionaries started mission work in Borneo.

The first missionaries from the AGUSA, Cecil and Edith Jackson, arrived in Singapore in 1928, and in Malaya in 1932.. In 1930, Esther Johnson and Carrie Anderson, followed by Katherine Clause in 1931, came to Singapore before starting their work in Malaya. Anderson was the first missionary to Malaya, and she began a Cantonese work among the Chinese at 4th Mile, Ampang Road, Kuala Lumpur, in 1934, with two new Chinese converts, and founded the First Assemblies of God, Kuala Lumpur, the oldest existing AGM church.

In 1936, Arthur E. Sandhal and his wife Esther Johnson arrived and pastored the church until 1949. Evangelists and some local youths formed a Tent Evangelistic Team and held evangelistic rallies in 1937–38, and many new believers were added to the church. In 1940, the church was officially registered and affiliated to the AGUSA. The Assemblies of God of Malaya and Singapore (AGMS) was officially organised on the occasion of the first General Council in 1957, reformed in 1966, and celebrated its Golden Jubilee in 2007. The early

AG mission works were concentrated on the western coast of West Malaysia and only started limited church-planting efforts on the eastern coast in 1977 in view of the Islamic dominance in the Malay states.

Besides AGUSA missionaries in Malaya, the Finnish Free Foreign Mission of Pentecostal Churches of Finland had started mission works on the eastern coast of Malaya after the Second World War. The Australian Borneo Evangelical Mission had played an important role in extensive indigenous mission works since 1928 in the interior of Sarawak. Their 'Three-Self' indigenous church, Sidang Injil Borneo, was established in 1959 and became the fastest-growing church in East Malaysia among the *Orang Ulu*.

The Ceylon Pentecostal Mission started mission work among the Indian and Ceylonese (now Sri Lankan) migrant workers in Malaya in 1930 by A.K. Titus in Ipoh and Mr and Mrs V.V. Samuel in Kuala Lumpur. The Pentecostal Church of Malaya was registered in 1952 and began work among the Chinese in Penang in the 1950s. In 2000, there were around 1,000–1,500 members and 13 centres.

Notably, John Sung (1901–1944), an evangelist of the Methodist Church in Fujian, China, educated in America, conducted revival meetings in China and among the Chinese in Southeast Asia. He had phenomenal influence in major towns in Malaysia and Singapore from 1935 to 1940. He formed evangelistic bands for prayer and witness which were still active in the 1980s. Spontaneous prayers in John Sung's revival meetings were common among the Chinese churches, mainly Methodist and Presbyterian, and created openness to Charismatics and Pentecostalism. Kong Mui Yee, a Hong Kong actress, ministered in Malaysia and Singapore much later in 1963. Her evangelistic rallies and

Pentecostal teaching on Baptism in the Holy Spirit and speaking in tongues had stirred some opposition among the Chinese due to her condemning the Chinese religious practices. She was initially invited by the AGMS but soon disassociated when she started her own churches under the New Testament Church movement.

These early missionaries had done the groundwork which had helped create the distinctiveness of Malaysian Pentecostalism. The AGUSA missionaries did not come into a spiritual vacuum. The early mission presence and Pentecostal revival ministries had contributed to the unique Malaysian Pentecostal spirituality and theology, which are not identical with the AGUSA's.

The Inception Period

The early Pentecostal foreign missionary community of the AGM led the movement for 40 years. Local leadership emerged in 1974 with the first Malaysian general superintendent, Prince Guneratnam (1974–2000), followed by Vincent Leoh (2000–2008) and Ong Sek Leang (2008–present).

A significant contributing factor to the expansion of the Pentecostal movement was the founding of the Bible College of Malaysia (formerly known as the Bible Institute of Malaya), the AGM's own Pentecostal Bible college to train and raise up local ministers engaged in local missions, church planting, and church ministry in Malaysia and Singapore. Founded by Delmer and Eleanor Guynes, missionaries to Malaysia in 1952 to 1964, the first lecturers were American missionaries. The first 12 students were recruited from Penang, Raub, Kuala Lumpur, and Singapore.

From 1974 to 2000, the total number of churches increased almost sevenfold, from 43 to 301, membership from 2,000 to 33,662, and adherents from around 3,400 to 47,073. Many church senior pastors, pastors, and leaders of para-church organisations and missionary movements are Bible College of Malaysia (BCM) graduates. In 1972, Malaysia Tamil Bible Institute, a sister Bible school, was founded, and about 90% of the Tamil work was led by ministers who graduated from there.

The AGM's church planting was mainly in the urban areas using English, Chinese, and Tamil languages, and much later the Malay language, in the 1980s. The Pentecostal and (later) Charismatic movement that swept across Malaysia has been strong on mission and church planting, and the new churches are identified as 'Spirit-filled', 'Charismatic', or 'Pentecostal'. The churches that emerged in these pioneer movements identify themselves with an emphasis on the Holy Spirit. Over half a century, many young people received Spirit-baptism in youth camps and crusade meetings, and these powerful moves of the Holy Spirit have brought many into full-time ministry.

The Transition Period

Alongside the Pentecostal movement in Malaysia and the establishment of the AGM, the Charismatic movements and spiritual renewals were also happening simultaneously among all other denominations in Malaysia from the mid-1970s to 1990s.

The Fountain Trust, which was founded in 1964 in the United Kingdom, was a vehicle in spreading the Charismatic movement and spiritual renewal in Singapore, Sabah, Sarawak, and Peninsular Malaysia in the 1970s. The Charismatic renewal in the Anglican Church in Malaysia came through an Anglican priest from England, Peter Young, who organised 'The Renewal Fellowship' in 1974. The non-denominational fellowship attracted people from the AG, Methodists, Lutherans, and Brethren from Petaling Jaya Gospel Hall.

In 1975, the Roman Catholic Church in Malaysia joined this Renewal Fellowship Council, making all denominations in Malaysia represented as the Charismatic movement swept across Malaysia. Many spiritual renewal conferences were conducted in major state capitals throughout the country. The Charismatic movement peaked from mid-1970s through 1990s throughout Malaysia. The AGM was an expanding Pentecostal movement, spreading and growing rapidly during this period of Charismatic Movement.

In 2020, the AGM had 393 churches, 49,810 adherents and 823 credentialed members, in geographically defined ecclesiastical groupings, organised into six and later seven districts. Other AG mission works in Asia have many similarities with the history of the AGM.

Conclusion

The outpouring of the Spirit as prophesied in Joel 2 and fulfilled in Acts 2 has been phenomenal, particularly in the global Pentecostalism, Spirit renewals, and revivals in past centuries. Although the AGM's contextualised Pentecostalism, theological emphases, and practices change over six decades, the centrality of Joel 2–Acts 2 remains the essence of contemporary Pentecostal spirituality.

Chapter Two
Key Theological Themes of Pentecostalism: Joel 2 and Acts 2

The main beliefs and practices of the AG originated from the two foundational texts, Joel 2 and Acts 2. Baptism in the Holy Spirit is the primary Pentecostal experience and doctrine, from which other key Pentecostal distinctives are derived.

The early Pentecostals had a living reality of the outpouring of the Spirit from Joel's prophecy and Acts 2, particularly in the Azusa Street revival in the early twentieth century, and theologised their spiritual experiences from these texts. They were 'biblicists' and believed that their experience was based solidly on Scripture.

Baptism in the Holy Spirit

Baptism in the Holy Spirit is synonymous with Spirit-baptism or being filled with the Holy Spirit, which means to be immersed in the Holy Spirit. This signifies a total submergence within the reality of the Holy Spirit, so that whoever is so baptised has a vivid sense of the Spirit's presence and power.

For Pentecostals, Baptism in the Holy Spirit is the fulfilment of Joel's prophecy: 'I will pour out my Spirit' on the Day of Pentecost, as explained by Peter (Acts 2). We cannot understand the Pentecostal experience without locating it in the doctrine of Baptism in the Holy Spirit. Described by Macchia as 'the crown jewel of Pentecostal distinctives', it 'remains the very substance of the church's life in the Spirit, including its charismatic life and mission'. Pentecostals believe that Baptism in the Holy Spirit results in empowerment, based on Acts 1:8. The power for service includes the gifts of the Spirit (especially the 'nine gifts' in 1 Cor. 12).

In the development of a more holistic understanding of Baptism in the Holy Spirit, the central doctrine in Pentecostal theology, contemporary theologians argue that it has a broader meaning and theological significance than empowerment for service in Luke-Acts. They extend its boundaries to encompass regeneration, sacramentalism, empowerment, sanctification, koinonia, and eschatology, emphasising that Baptism in the Holy Spirit should be understood from the Pauline pneumatology in salvation, '*being* in Christ', and the source of empowerment in living witness is '*functioning* in Christ in the power of the Spirit'.

Glossolalia

Glossolalia is 'the religious phenomenon of making sounds that constitute, or resemble, a language not known to the speaker'. Glossolalia is the initial physical sign of the Baptism in the Holy Spirit. In Acts 2:17-18, speaking in tongues is specifically described as a fulfilment of Joel's prophecy that in the last days all of God's people will prophesy. Glossolalia is 'inspired speech associated with worship and prophetic pronouncements'.

Early Pentecostal Understanding – Xenolalia

Early Pentecostals linked speaking in tongues to mission, which had directly spurred the worldwide Pentecostal movement, and believed that speaking in tongues was xenolalia (the gift of foreign language) to preach the gospel to the world in the 'last days', through which the recipients' mission fields were identified. In the Azusa Street revival in 1906, *The Apostolic Faith* reported on xenolalia after receiving Baptism in the Holy Spirit: 'Many have spoken in the languages of India, China, Africa, Asia, Europe, and the islands of the sea, as well as the learned languages of Greek and Latin.' God was calling new-tongued missionaries to different parts of the world and the Spirit giving utterance were signs to the heathen of God's message.

Just within two years, Azusa Street revival missions had reached 25 nations, and more than 200 Pentecostal missionaries had been sent abroad by 1910. The direct role of glossolalia in mission was the belief that new Spirit-missionaries did not have to go through language-learning.

Classical Understanding – Glossolalia

In the turning of the first decade the majority of Pentecostals abandoned the belief of xenolalia and switched to the belief in glossolalia (unknown tongues) as the 'evidence' of Baptism in the Holy

Spirit, after missionary failures when hearers could not understand the foreign tongues. As the focus on crisis eschatology and xenolalia waned, the emphasis on the doctrine of speaking in tongues repositioned to glossolalia as the initial evidence of Baptism in the Holy Spirit. Both Baptism in the Holy Spirit and glossolalia have roots in wider Christian spirituality and Christian tradition centuries earlier.

All Flesh

The Apostolic Faith reported on the Azusa Street revival that many women with the gift of tongues were anointed preachers and missionaries. The Wesleyan-Holiness spirituality encouraged women to be included in ministries, such as prophetic ministry, and in missions as well, before the turn of the twentieth century. The Holy Spirit had anointed, empowered, and bestowed charismatic gifts on women the same as on men as leaders, pioneers, preachers, and missionaries worldwide, especially in the early years of Pentecostalism in North America, the USA, and majority world. Many women were called and commissioned and played significant and prominent roles in the widespread of Pentecostalism in the missionary movement, and were involved as elders, pioneers, evangelists in healing movements, preachers with signs and wonders, and educators in Pentecostal Bible schools.

The AG granted full ordination to women in 1935. However, in the second half of the century, women's roles in leadership began to decline drastically and be minimised, due to the reality of patriarchalism, sexism, promotion of subordination to men, and cultural oppression which women have had to struggle with and endure in many countries. Contemporary Pentecostals are becoming more aware of promoting women's rights, sexual equality, and a more egalitarian practice, thus expressing a truer freedom in the Spirit.

The Return of Christ

The belief for many early Pentecostals was that the coming of the Spirit 'in the last days' meant that they were living near the time of the second coming of Christ. In more structured ways, these eschatological messages formed the early Pentecostal thought and worldview which initiated movements such as Full Gospel, Latter Rain, Apostolic Faith, and Pentecostal, and became their earlier doctrinal themes. The following were the central eschatological messages of the early Pentecostals.

'The Everlasting Gospel' and 'This Gospel of the Kingdom'

The central Pentecostal message of the return of Christ was supported by the wedding imagery. The early Pentecostal movement was directed by the Lord's last call to preach the gospel to the world, and heralded the 'midnight cry', 'Behold, the Bridegroom cometh, go ye out to meet him.' The twofold mission was the warning to awaken the church to join the wedding preparation and set the early Pentecostal expectations for evangelising the world before it was too late. A creative link about joining the wedding preparation was that believers must receive the 'wedding ring' or 'seal of the Holy Spirit', which was Baptism in the Holy Spirit with the evidence of glossolalia or 'speaking in unknown tongues'.

'The Latter Rain' Doctrine

The Pentecostal revival began as the restoration of the apostolic faith and had its roots in 'The Latter Rain' doctrine of early Pentecostal belief. The early Pentecostals understood that the original Pentecost in Acts 2 was the early rain, and that the outpouring of the Spirit in Pentecostalism as the latter rain would restore the church to how it was in the early apostolic church, as in the book of Acts. Just as in the apostolic era, there was the restoration of the ninefold gifts of the Spirit in the last days and the supernatural elements of the New Testament, such as signs and wonders, miracles, divine healing, and 'supernatural gifts of the Spirit', in preparation for the harvest and the return of Christ. Early Pentecostals justified that God is unchanging and therefore the nature of the apostolic church was claimed to be normative at all times.

'The Latter Rain' doctrine gave the early Pentecostals a coherent explanation to link together their understanding of 'the last days', revival, the outpouring of the Spirit or the spiritual emergence of 'Pentecostalism', the restoration of 'Apostolic Faith', 'God's dispensational plan for the ages', and the expectation of the imminent return of Christ. These were all expressed in the four elements of the 'fourfold gospel' (Jesus as saviour, Spirit-baptizer, healer and coming king) or 'full gospel'. Contemporary Pentecostals believe that Peter's phrase 'the last days' (Acts 2:17) means 'the entire period between the first and second advents of Christ'.

The Missionary Emphasis

After the Second World War, there were substantial shifts from the early Pentecostals' crisis eschatology and missionary fervour to other theological motivations for missions. Billy Graham became a prominent evangelist in 1948. At the same time, the 'prosperity gospel' based on 3 John 2, or the 'Word of Faith Movement', became a widespread theology of hope for America's post-war society as the post-Depression economy improved with a new prosperity trend. Oral Roberts also became a prominent evangelist and started TV evangelism in 1953, and his salvation-healing crusades had drawn many Pentecostals. After this, many prosperity gospel preachers have emerged. However, the AGUSA was against many teachings of prosperity gospel and advised believers to consider the total teaching of Scripture.

The Pentecostal interpretation and understanding of Joel 2 and Acts 2 have changed over the century. Ultimately, it is the Holy Spirit that motivates missions, thus the importance of Baptism in the Holy Spirit as the empowerment for witness, and the sending Spirit as in Joel–Acts is the fundamental driving force of the Pentecostals, made possible by the Spirit's empowerment.

Revivalism

Revival is the outpouring of the Holy Spirit upon God's people in vast measure, just as Joel has prophesied in Joel 2:28-32 and fulfilled on the Day of Pentecost in Acts 2. In the last 50 years, there have been several revivals, including Brownsville Assembly of God (1995–2000), Toronto Airport (1994), and healing crusades by Reinhard Bonnke and Benny Hinn in Africa, India, and other parts of the world, as well as Hillsong and Bethel today, which are classical Pentecostal or Charismatic, the newer development. In the twenty-first century, contemporary Pentecostals globally continue to yearn for revival from time to time, when the Pentecostal spirituality begins to plateau or dampen and the church is losing her spiritual vitality and mission emphasis.

Revivalism, whether in early or contemporary Pentecostalism, is crucial to the life of the believers and the community/church to remain faithful to God in carrying out the missionary tasks in the power of the Holy Spirit. Revivalism always restores intimate relationships with the triune God and ignites the missionary zeal.

Prophecies, Dreams, and Visions

Spirit-given prophecies, dreams, and visions are part of God's promise in Joel's prophecy that all people, regardless of age, gender, and social status, can be filled with His presence and have direct communication and revelation from God by the indwelling of the Holy Spirit. In Acts and the church era, Spirit-baptised believers receive gifts of the Holy Spirit, most prominently the gift of prophecy, as all can prophecy, dream, and see visions. In the Old Testament, dreams and visions were elements of prophecy, and their fulfilment in Acts 2 marks a significant change from the endowment of the Holy Spirit on only a few chosen individuals in the Old Testament, to the prophethood of all believers as the Holy Spirit comes upon all flesh.

The term 'Voice of the Spirit' has been used since early Pentecostalism in the 1900s to describe the ways of divine revelations and messages inspired by the Holy Spirit, in the various forms of prophecies, visions, and dreams, the audible voice of God, and inward witness. Since the early Pentecostal revival, the Voice of the Spirit in a broader sense was practically expressed through the gift of tongues followed by interpretation, a word in a known language, in Scripture, sermon, prophecy, vision, dream, song, prayer, and benediction.

Early Pentecostals viewed the gifts of tongues and Spirit-given prophecies, dreams, and visions as part of the evidence of the latter rain: 'Christ is making up His jewels quickly. O how the "latter rain" is falling.' *The Apostolic Faith* newsletters during the Azusa Street revival reported that many messages from God were given through prophecies spoken in unknown tongues with interpretation, and prophecies, dreams, and visions were received by many who were Spirit-baptised, regardless of age, gender, nationality, and social background. Most prophecies given through interpreted messages spoken in tongues and visions were apocalyptic: the premillennial returning of Christ, 'the end is near', the missionary urgency, healing, ministries, and personal life. And the visions received were mostly apocalyptic visions of Jesus, end times, hell and heaven, among others, which drove the eschatological fervour and missionary emphasis in early Pentecostalism.

Since early Pentecostalism, prophecies, dreams, and visions have been a significant channel through which God calls missionaries to foreign nations and how the Holy Spirit provides direction to the missionary endeavours and ministries.

The universal missionary endeavour of the Azusa Street mission has spread widely into many nations. The early AG missionary to Singapore and Malaya, Lula Ashmore (Mrs Lula Baird), received Christ in 1928 and was praying and speaking in tongues for three hours. She was touched by the Holy Spirit and received a specific call to Singapore. She heard the Voice of the Spirit and cried out over and over, 'Singapore, Singapore, Singapore', and was convinced that she was called for mission to the Chinese. She learned Mandarin and Cantonese in Hong Kong and arrived at Singapore in 1939 and Malaya in 1940.

Contemporary Understanding

Prophecies, dreams, and visions continue to play an essential role in contemporary Pentecostal spirituality, and in the Holy Spirit providing direction to contemporary Pentecostals in missions, churches, ministries, and personal lives.

Conclusion

Joel's prophecy and its fulfilment in Acts 2 have been the foundational scriptures for the Pentecostal movement since the Topeka Pentecost in 1901 and the Azusa Street revival in 1906, followed by the worldwide revivals over the past century until the present.

The early Pentecostals' missional motivation, which made Pentecostalism the worldwide missionary movement, has gradually faded with the development of the new eschatological perspective of salvation history. Baptism in the Holy Spirit as empowerment for mission remains core to Pentecostal spirituality, with new missional frontiers and approaches. The Holy Spirit is the missionary Spirit, and contemporary Pentecostal spirituality continues to emphasise revivalism to renew the spiritual vitality of the Pentecostal community in order to carry on its mission to fulfil the Great Commission and world evangelism. Prophecies, dreams, and visions remain core in Pentecostal spirituality in missions, churches, ministries, and personal lives.

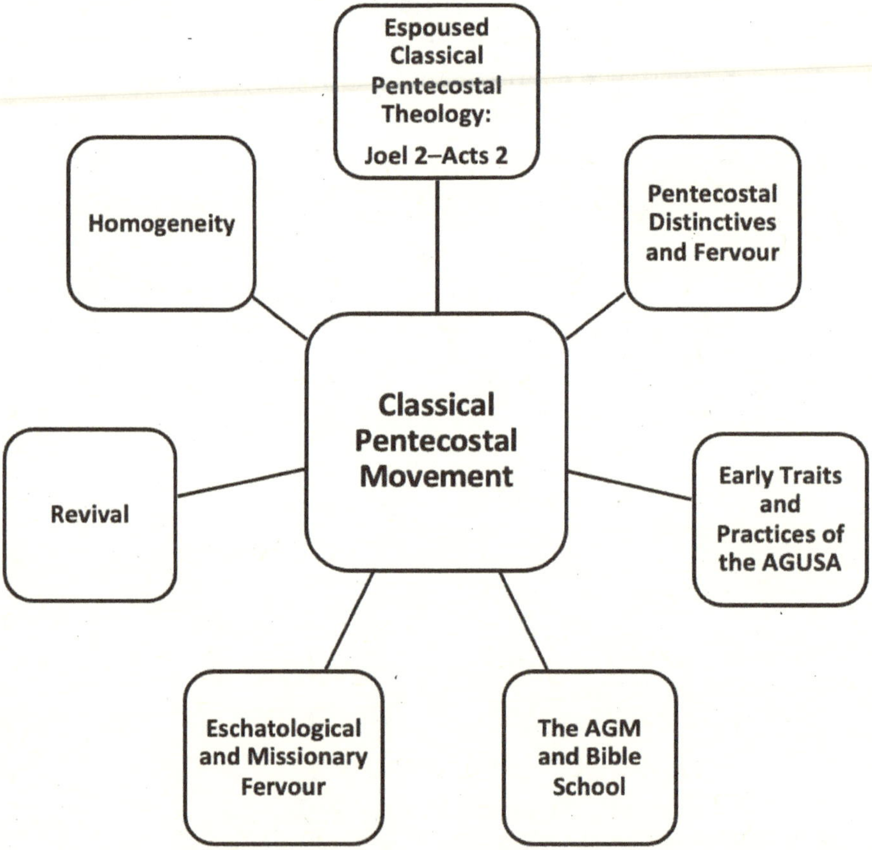

Figure 1: Classical formation 1957–1974 – classical emphases

Chapter Three
Stage 1 – The Situation and Its Complexities

Classical Formation (1957–1974)

The fellowship of the AGMS was officially recognised on 6 February 1957 with the formation of the General Council, and separated into two entities in 1966 following the political separation of Malaysia and Singapore the previous year.

The classical emphases are shown in Figure 1 opposite.

Espoused Classical Pentecostal Theology: Joel 2–Acts 2

The AGM has inherited its classical Pentecostal theology and practices from early missionaries of the AGUSA. The theological themes derived from Joel 2–Acts 2 are fundamental to understand the AGM's theology and practices as illustrated in Figure 2 overleaf, where from the central Pentecostal distinctive of Baptism in the Holy Spirit flow other distinctives, emphases, and practices.

In the formative period of the AGM in the 1960s and 1970s, there were many revival meetings and 'tarrying meetings'. These were long

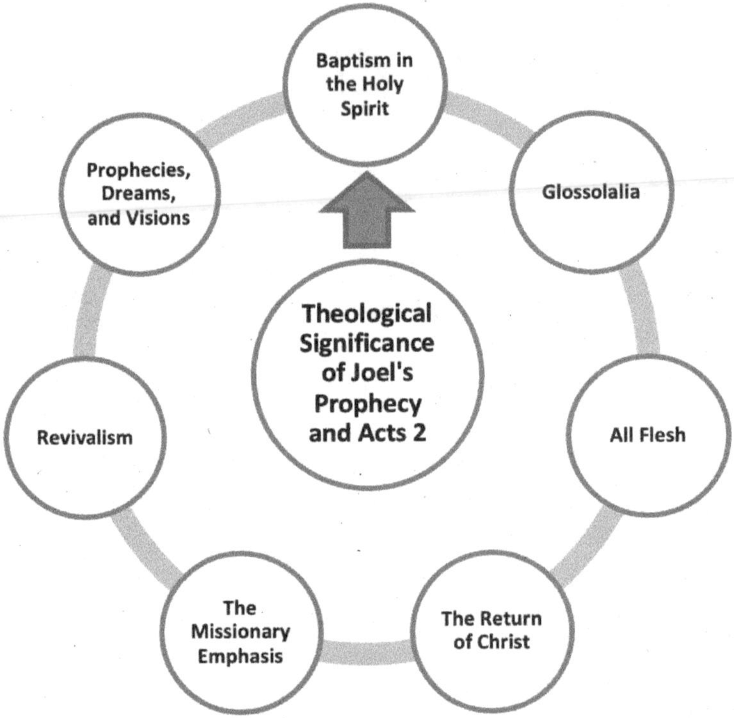

Figure 2: Key theological themes of Joel 2–Acts 2

services in the presence of the Holy Spirit, where many received the Baptism in the Holy Spirit and spiritual gifts, with the evangelistic zeal and passion. On the other hand, the AGM also inherited some Western baggage which led to some downsides and was later disengaged with, such as legalistic holiness.

Alongside church planting, revival meetings, evangelistic rallies, and so on, Bible schools were part of the AGUSA's 'DNA'. As the AG missionaries needed to train local workers, the Bible Institute of Malaya was established on 3 January 1960, starting with a three-year diploma programme. The first graduating class was in 1962 with seven graduates. The AG's Bible school is one of the most successful and lasting Pentecostal missionary works established by the early missionaries. The Bible Institute of Malaya was renamed the Bible College of Malaysia in 1982, and had her 60th anniversary in 2020, and Pentecostal theological education continues to play a vital role in the process of contextualisation.

Eschatological and Missionary Fervour

The theological link between Spirit-baptism and missions had been lived out by the early AG missionaries and pioneers of the AGM movement until the mid-1980s. This primary theological focus was also transmitted to the nationals so that they became mission-oriented from the outset. The early Pentecostal emphasis was on eschatology, thus the sense of passion for the kingdom. In fact, the AGM started as a youth movement, and many early church planters were filled with zeal and boldness to do 'house-to-house evangelism' or 'door-to-door evangelism'.

One significant practice of the AG in its services and meetings is the altar-call ministry. It is during altar calls that salvation and healing take place, when many are convicted by the Holy Spirit, Spirit-baptised, and respond to God's call for service, missions, and ministry.

The AGM was strongly impacted by the waves of revival that were sweeping across the region during the formative period, which heightened the eschatological and missionary emphasis. Missionary reports and magazines confirm the first outpouring of the Holy Spirit throughout Malaysia and Singapore in the late 1950s, and the Youth Camp in 1960 was said to be the biggest ever, with well over 200 young people registered.

In the 1960s and 1970s, the revival swept across Malaysia and surrounding countries as well. People were spiritually hungry and responsive to God and the work of the Holy Spirit. There was a harvest of souls and revival among the youths as many gathered to pray and seek God and many were filled with the Holy Spirit, with a tremendous increase over the next decade.

Since the transition of leadership from AG missionaries to the national leadership of Guneratnam as the first Malaysian AG General Superintendent in 1974 (he was Assistant General Superintendent in 1973), the major missional strategy for growth has been the intensity of the Bible school's mission in raising local pioneers and ministers for church-planting endeavours. The tremendous growth spurts had resulted in the AGM becoming a strong influence in spearheading the Spirit-filled Christian landscape in the nation. The Pentecostals had grown rapidly from 5,440 in 1960 to 61,500 adherents in 1985, which made up 13.6% of Christians in Malaysia, whereas Evangelicals are 17.5%, others 15.2%, and the largest denomination being the Roman Catholics at 53.7%.

The AGM's national leadership under Guneratnam was a smooth transition from the AG missionaries. The spiritual atmosphere of revival was still ongoing. There was a stronger and more intense focus on Bible school training of local youths who responded to God's call during the 'youth revival' in the late 1970s and early 1980s, and the raising of many local pioneers, pastors, missionaries, and evangelists for the field.

The intense emphasis on evangelism and church planting from the labour and fruits of Bible schools was evident in the exponential growth in pioneering work and church-planting endeavours, as consistent batches of pioneers and ministers were launched out into the harvest field. There was growth from the 1970s and 1980s, followed by slower but steady growth to the present time. By June 2000, the AGM had 325 churches with 45,000 adherents and active social ministries of six drug rehabilitation centres and 18 social homes.

The explosive growth of the AGM in the 1970s peaked in the mid-1980s, making it the fastest-growing church movement in the country, and the AGM became a strong influence spearheading the Spirit-filled Christian landscape in the nation. Complexities began from the mid-1980s onward with a shift in emphases. In the 1980s through to the 50th anniversary in 2007 the AGM has grown large and strong, and outward expansion has stabilised.

The movement's vast expansion resulted in a shift of emphasis as illustrated in Figure 3 overleaf.

The first changing nature in the establishment of the AGM is the contextualisation of the Pentecostal movement from a Western American Pentecostal movement to a Malaysian Pentecostal movement over the decades, when the early missionaries had returned to their home countries and the AGM came under national leadership from 1974 onward. One aspect of the shifts was the

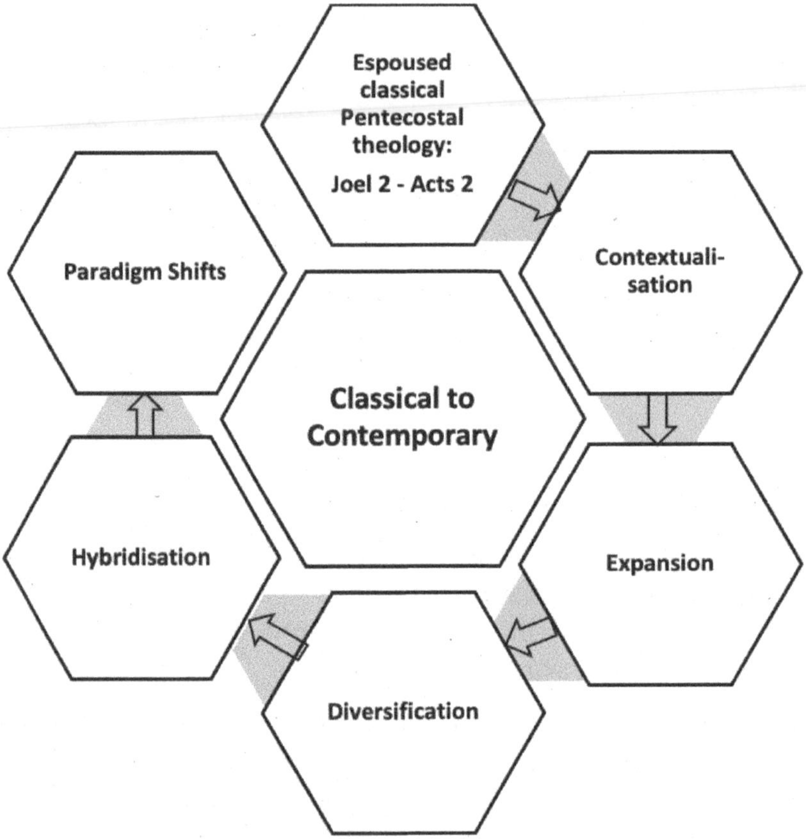

Figure 3: Classical to contemporary – complexities in changing nature and shifts in emphases (classical Pentecostal movement homogeneity until the mid-1980s)

difference between the perspectives that were learned and perspectives in grassroots realities. There were shifts in the missionary perspectives to actual practices when engaging with local or native cultures, traditions, ways of life, socioeconomy, animistic religious beliefs, and so forth. These were assimilated into the Malaysians' multicultural and multireligious setting, which had become more visible from the 1980s onward.

The AGM reached a new phase where churches had begun to grow larger and were more organised. It was a season of maturing, with a growing need to nurture the spiritual growth of the members and build spiritual foundations within the churches. As a result, there was more focus on building up the church and members in more holistic aspects of Christian living. Gradually, churches became wealthier and more established, leaders and pastors became more widely accepted by society and by other Evangelicals, the preaching and teaching in churches covered a wider range of topics instead of revolving only around Spirit-baptism and missions, as was the case in the 1970s. Many churches were planted in most towns and adherents grew in numbers.

The shift in focus to church growth was good and necessary, and the movement also grew in multilingual congregations, particularly Chinese, Tamil, and the national language. From the 2000s, the national leadership saw the need to pass on the Pentecostal heritage to the next generation.

The third main changing nature of the AGM is the diversification of theological, missional, church, and ministerial focus and emphases. Many preaching and teaching resources which can be easily accessed are not purely Pentecostal. There is also diversification in missional emphases in terms of strategies, methods, and approaches, church programmes, and ministerial aspects. There is more diversification in social-concern works and other forms of missions and evangelism, with increasing social-concern ministries like homes for orphans and underprivileged children, drug rehabilitation centres, senior citizen homes, and kidney dialysis centres.

The fourth main changing nature is the hybridisation of theological influences from the Evangelicals, Charismatics, Third Wave, and the Independent Network Charismatic. Generally, Pentecostals are an active member of the National Evangelical Christian Fellowship. At the same time, because of the common spiritual experiences of Baptism in the Holy Spirit, the AGM is also closely affiliated with the Charismatics. There is also a sense of unity among Malaysian churches as the distinctions are getting more blended.

This main factor in the hybridisation of external theology has shifted to a blend of theology from hyper-charismatic Third Wave beliefs which have made inroads into the AGM over time, especially from mid-1980s onward. The fruits of the global Third Wave spiritual renewal also resulted in the emerging Fourth Wave in present times.

The conceptualised themes in the 'movement growth' period have impacted the practices of contemporary Pentecostalism in the Malaysian context, as the AGM has morphed from a classical Pentecostal movement toward modernisation. The 'Contemporary Pentecostal Church Movement' marks the beginning of the AGM's new image, engaging the young generation and employing different methodologies and necessary tools in bringing the message (gospel) across, while maintaining the Malaysian culture.

The Executive Committee embraces this new identity of the AGM movement to bring a sense of freshness, new outlook, and moving with the times to engage the present generation. AGM leadership affirms that the Contemporary Pentecostal Church Movement's espoused theology has not changed, but its image, outlook, methods, and practices have. The centrality of the espoused classical Pentecostal theology (based on Joel 2–Acts 2) preserves the Pentecostal heritage, as illustrated in the following Figure 4.

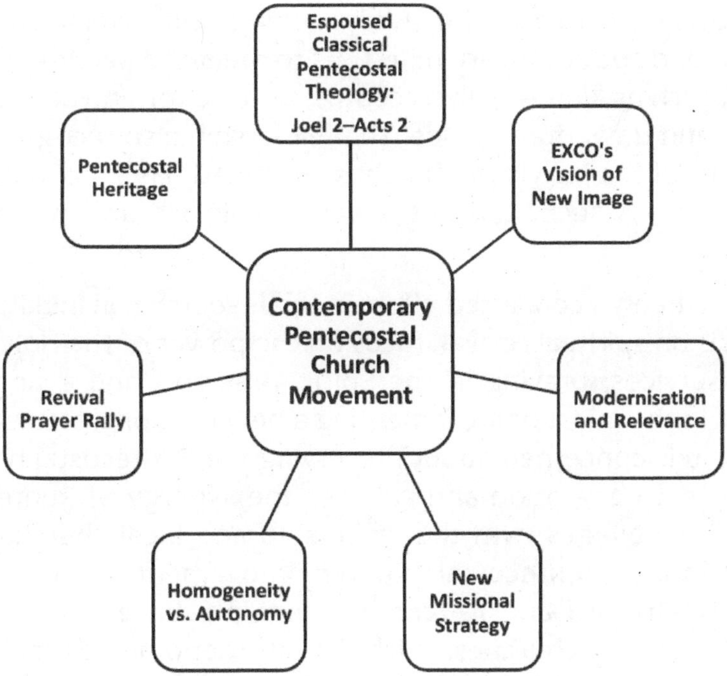

Figure 4: 'A Contemporary Pentecostal Church Movement': The AGM's official tagline, 2018 (Executive Committee's desired contemporary emphases)

In present times, a contemporary outlook is vital in modern society to continue to be relevant to the present community and younger generations. One of the most visible changes would be the use of modern media for the effective proclamation of the gospel message in this modern age. And it has got to be embraced by all AGM churches in order to be effective, while maintaining a Malaysian Pentecostal identity and flavour.

As a movement, the General Council is again encouraging church planting, especially in smaller towns, villages, and new neighbourhood areas, with a broadening and diversification of missions and social concern ministries to meet the needs of today's society, such as kidney dialysis centres and aid for unwed pregnant women and unwanted babies. The leadership also recognises the autonomy of the individual churches, as the AGM is a fellowship and movement. As such, there is a variance in vibrancy within the movement.

There has been a concerted effort in the leadership in initiating the emphasis on spiritual revival, focus on the power of the Holy Spirit, revival services, praying in the Spirit, missions, and evangelistic fervour. In the midst of implementing a new missional strategy, the leadership is concerned about preserving the Pentecostal heritage for the next generation and stresses the synergy of Pentecostal theological colleges with the leadership and local churches. The contemporary Pentecostal Church movement also strongly emphasises 'revival' and prayer movement in a concerted effort with other Malaysian churches, such as interdenominational Prayer United and National Evangelical Christian Fellowship.

Voice of the Spirit

The Voice of the Spirit is a significant part of the AGM's historical development as it demonstrates an implicit theology and practice shaped by Joel's prophecy, which has impacted the AGM's growth and development from classical to contemporary. Although prophecies, dreams, and visions have not been a primary topic in the AGM's preaching or teaching per se (as compared to the gospel, Baptism in the Holy Spirit, spiritual gifts, missions, and other aspects of Christian faith), the many testimonies from interviews and surveys reveal that receiving prophecies, dreams, and visions or hearing the Voice of the Spirit are an essential practice in the spirituality of many AGM ministers, particularly in their calling to ministry and being led by the Spirit in missions, church, and ministry.

The Voice of the Spirit as divine revelation from the Holy Spirit in prophecies, dreams, and visions is a striking theological theme from Joel's prophecy in the AGM, and it is different from the Asian religiosity, where dreams and visions play a significant role. Many Pentecostal testimonies show that usually the call to full-time ministry is preceded by some kind of hearing of God's voice through visions and dreams: some kind of direct divine intervention. There is an underlying theology that comes out of Joel – a special understanding of divine intervention. This pattern in Joel shapes the practice of AGM ministers, especially in their call to ministry, that something supernatural is to be relived.

The idea and nature of prophecies, dreams, and visions also have gone through an evolution over time, from a more literal and vivid imagery, e.g. of Christ, heaven, hell, cross, and etc. in the 1960s and

1970s, to a more metaphoric and conceptual nature, such as dreams and envisioning. There are changes in ideas and the nature of prophecies, dreams, and visions practised in the AGM, influenced by the different ethos from the First Wave (Pentecostal), Second Wave (Charismatic renewal) to Third Wave (Neo-Charismatic Movement) from the classical formation period to present times. There is also the change in the concept and meaning of dreams and visions by modern management influence, where now churches have vision and mission statements, just like business corporations. Mutually, the church is influencing the world and the secular world is influencing the church.

Prophecies, dreams, and visions remain instrumental in the calling of ministers. Consistent with earlier periods, about over one-third of respondents received their call during their personal time with God in devotions, worship, and prayer, while two-thirds received it at camps and meetings, and during sermons and altar calls.

Ministers are being led by the Holy Spirit in new ways, approaches, and directions at different times and seasons. Their sensitivity, attentiveness, and obedience to the Holy Spirit's leading and direction in life, missions, and service are instrumental in the AGM's tremendous growth over six decades from just a few churches to almost 400 today, with diversified, social-concerned ministries impacting cities and communities.

Ministerial Practices

In the classical formation and pioneering period, there were strong emphases on salvation, Baptism in the Holy Spirit, glossolalia, and empowerment for life and service, evangelism and missions. However, from the mid-1980s onward, there has been a strong emphasis on Baptism in the Holy Spirit for body ministry, personal prophecy, and moving in the gifts of the Holy Spirit, power healing, power encounter, and power evangelism, especially from the Charismatic and Third Wave influence. The Voice of the Spirit plays significant role in the AGM's growth, particularly in guiding AGM ministers in God's calling, missiology, ecclesiology, and ministerial aspects from the pioneering to the contemporary period.

Many pioneers were in their youth when they received God's call during the classical formation period. There is a difference in the nature and form of prophecies, dreams, and visions received by the older generation as compared to those received by the new generation today, as evidenced by their testimonies.

In seeking God, there is a difference between the early Pentecostal practice of 'tarrying', in waiting on the Holy Spirit, and the more contemporary Third Wave's International House of Prayer method of soaking in God's presence and enjoying the time of worship, prayer, and intercession; namely, the 'Harp and Bowl model'. Whether the International House of Prayer falls into the Third Wave category is a matter of debate. The practice may be different, but the Holy Spirit speaks and the people receive prophecies, visions, impressions, and promptings of the Holy Spirit. Although the methods and practices used by some AGM ministers may have changed, the Holy Spirit still ministers and speaks to God's people, who gather to seek His face, worship Him in spirit and in truth, and wait upon Him.

In ministerial aspects, from the 1980s there has been a stronger focus on the Voice of the Spirit in the widely varying ministerial practices in AGM churches, especially in prayer and intercession, preaching, altar calls, and general ministering to people. Given the change of meaning over time, a prophetic word can mean God's word and message given through the written Word of God, thoughts, impressions, or prompting by the Holy Spirit for His specific purpose which will be fulfilled.

The Third Wave's prophetic movement has introduced many new kinds of prophecies, dreams, and visions, and new parlance; namely, 'personal prophecy', 'confirmation', 'releasing' the prophetic word, and 'inner vision'. These are propagated by a global network of 'prophets' but are rare in early Pentecostalism. 'Specific prophecies' given in prophetic conferences have become a new kind of prophetic movement and a popular contemporary feature. All these have been made popular practices in the prophetic movement but are rare in early Pentecostalism.

Personal prophecies are also a new kind of prophecy, which can also be closely associated with the word of knowledge and wisdom for a specific person, situation, or place, in the present or the future.

'Release' is a new term in Pentecostal parlance, which is a more subtle kind of 'inner vision' and prophetic style. It carries certain theological connotations reflecting the spiritual technology of the Third Wave. Ministers receive and 'release' prophetic words for the people they pray for and minister to; these can be words of confirmation, edification, comfort, healing, assurance, or a simple Scripture.

Most times, the prophetic messages are being prompted by the Holy Spirit in the form of impressions, but these may not be in vivid images, but sometimes more like a gut feeling, an intuition with meanings or interpretations.

One conspicuous change in the interpretation of prophecies, dreams, and visions in the AGM over time is the form of literal imagery and words received by early Pentecostals and early pioneers of the AGM. But nowadays, the Voice of the Spirit is not necessarily in imagery form, but more commonly in the form of inner witness, a burden, prompting, desire or conceptual ideas, impressions, personal prophecies, or praying over people with instant revelations. This is a new phenomenon, where these new kinds of prophecies, dreams, and visions are enigmatic.

The Voice of the Spirit has been a significant spiritual element in the AGM's growth and development as a Spirit-led movement and community of faith.

In contemporary times, there is a tension between preserving the classical Pentecostal distinctives and staying in tune with cultural trends to make the gospel relevant. The new image of the contemporary Pentecostal Church movement and the leadership's contemporary emphases seek to minimise the gap between the espoused and the current practice in reviving the Pentecostal and missionary fervour. The nationwide synergy of the AGM and the Malaysian churches praying for revival in the nation recognises the importance of the centrality of Joel 2–Acts 2 in today's church. Even though times have changed, Pentecostal theological education continues to play a vital role in the AGM's contextualisation process and growth.

Chapter Four
Stage 2 – Contextual Analysis

Historical Factors

The historical background of the AGM's Pentecostalism can be traced from the roots of American Pentecostalism. The AGUSA became one of the largest Pentecostal movements, sending out missionaries to every part of the world, including Malaya and Singapore, as AGUSA Foreign Missions reported, in the first half to the middle of the twentieth century.

The establishment of the AG in this region had similar Pentecostal practices to early American Pentecostalism, and the main missional strategy of the AGUSA missionaries in many nations around the world was the establishment of the AG General Council and Pentecostal Bible schools to train and raise national leadership for the local field to plant and pastor churches.

From the 1970s, most foreign missionaries across all Christian denominations had to leave Malaysia due to the immigration restriction, and the movement passed on to Malaysian leadership in 1974. Today the AGM is Malaysian Pentecostal in its diverse ethnicity and culture, as emphasised by its leadership and pioneers. The urban multilingual congregations practise more modern and contemporary worship services as compared to churches in more remote areas, where missions, evangelism, and ministries are adapted in a more holistic approach to grassroots realities and perspectives, as influenced by local or indigenous cultures, traditions, ways of life, socioeconomy, animistic religious beliefs or background, and so on.

Asia and the Two-Thirds World understand the realities of the spirit world, especially in their 'folk religion' and power encounter, unlike much of the Western worldview that rejects the belief in Satan or demons, 'principalities and powers'. However, the Pentecostals, Charismatics, and 'Third Wavers' have brought a sensitivity to the spiritual world back into prominence, in which dreams and visions have their own place.

There has also been an increase in controversial global movements and hyper-charismatic influences, particularly in beliefs, teachings, and contemporary worship experiences, including lyrics which lack theological, doctrinal, and biblical truths. Most of the setbacks of these many global trends and movements are their overemphasis on a particular area of faith, teaching, or spiritual gifts. Most of the newer hyper-charismatic movements have millions of followers worldwide and are very invasive. And because these Third Wave, New Apostolic Revelation and Independent Network Charismatic movements have the commonality of Baptism in the Holy Spirit and spiritual gifts, their hyper-charismatic teachings, prosperity gospel, 'name it and claim it', and other excesses could dilute the Pentecostal spirituality.

As a result of the various changes in theological emphases and teachings, there are changes in spirituality, dynamism, and practical theology over the periods, including discontinuity in certain early classical Pentecostal practices, as follows: waiting upon the Holy Spirit or 'tarrying meetings', the holiness movement, disengaging with certain attitudes, cultural appendages and theological baggage from the AGUSA roots, an evangelistic approach like 'door-to-door evangelism', house-to-house evangelism', 'tracting', and 'open air meetings'.

There are shifts in the ways of praying, from 'tarrying meetings' to prayer meetings, prayer altar, and prayer movement. There are shifts from regular altar calls for Baptism in the Holy Spirit, and exercising glossolalia, interpretation of tongues, and spiritual gifts in the past, to singing in the Spirit in contemporary worship or not at all. There is also a shift to new trends of contemporary worship, such as worship concerts, conferences, and seminars, and most churches have performing arts and musical productions for Easter and Christmas as evangelistic events. Naturally, there is a drastic decline in the practice of the Pentecostal distinctives such as Baptism in the Holy Spirit, glossolalia, and missions in some churches due to the many other main emphases and focuses during the diversified movement-growth period.

Contemporary Blends of Global Culture

In contemporary times, pioneers and senior ministers have stated that there is much blending of Pentecostal, Charismatic, Third Wave, and non-Pentecostals, resulting in generational growth with less exposure to Pentecostal fervour.

The major shifts in theological emphases and focus have had a direct impact on preaching or sermon focus, teaching, and missions. There is a lack of direct impact of the theological emphases on the missional zeal and practices today, compared to the early period.

The contemporary focus is more on unity and church in nation-building. There is a broader range and variety of external influences, such as spiritual health, emotional health, and social values. There are many messages of prosperity, survival, and blessing, but these lack the gospel message. Although there is a re-emphasis on the praying for believers to receive Baptism in the Holy Spirit, and doing the ministry of God, there is generally a lack in mission focus for the congregation.

In the 2010s the AGM national leadership emphasised revival and evangelistic and healing rallies, and there has also been a strong focus on prayer movement, with prophetic prayer conferences on revival and prayer strategies. As these conferences and practices were organised, the impact of these newer theological influences and practices in churches varied with the autonomous status of churches in the fellowship.

However, there has been a shift in the theological motivation in missions from eschatological fervour to the new understanding of 'the last days' in hermeneutical development. The paradigm shift in missiology involves the theological shift in the purpose of Baptism in the Holy Spirit as empowerment for missions to more emphasis on spiritual gifts for the edification of believers and the body of Christ.

The paradigm shifts in theological and missional motivation over the decades from the eschatological fervour and Baptism in the Holy Spirit empowerment for life and service have impacted the methods and approaches of carrying out missions.

New Hermeneutical Developments in Eschatology

The shift in eschatological motivation for evangelism and mission from the 1980s is evident in the waning 'crisis eschatology' on 'the last days' and the 'second coming of Christ' and missionary fervour driven by this underlying motivation. Pentecostal practices like 'tarrying meetings' and evangelism approaches like 'door-to-door evangelism' were driven by 'crisis eschatology'.

The shift in the underlying theology of 'crisis' eschatological fervour in early Pentecostalism to modern theological interpretation on 'the last days' and 'the latter rain' has impacted the changes in missionary fervour and missional approach.

Classical Pentecostals claim the normative pattern of Baptism in the Holy Spirit and glossolalia as being the 'initial physical evidence', thus believing there is a distinction between tongues as a 'sign' or initial evidence of Baptism in the Holy Spirit and as a 'gift' (1 Cor. 12:30; 14:5, 18), in relation to Paul's epistles to the Corinthians. From the earliest days of Pentecostalism, Holiness Pentecostals linked Baptism in the Holy Spirit with holiness, and only secondarily with missions. The early Pentecostals' view on Baptism in the Holy Spirit was narrowly focused on Acts or Lukan pneumatology. Some pioneers argued that the Charismatic influence since the 1980s had caused the decline on missional emphasis due to the different focus of Spirit-filled believers on spiritual gifts and edification within the body of Christ.

In the postmodern period, churches are generally becoming centripetal and modal in nature. These are global changes of missional emphasis which are prevalent in the world of Christianity today. In this modern time, churches need a balance of good structure and to be intentionally missional-focused in the midst of diversified emphases, as well as to mobilise a more holistic approach in missions and evangelism, particularly in reaching out and impacting the community.

Despite a different understanding of 'the last days' and the eschatological fervour of the formative period, Pentecostal missionary emphasis is not diminished. There have been new missional methods, approaches, perspectives, ideas, and strategies, and more specific roles in the contemporary period to suit the changing times and generations, as well as the Malaysian sociopolitical context.

Shift in Mission Ownership

The paradigm shift in missions is mainly the shift in responsibility from Spirit-baptised believers to mission organisations and mission departments of churches, as well as the diversification of mission field. As a result, the modus operandi of missions has changed drastically and many classical ways of doing missions have been discontinued. This has impacted the individual zeal and passion for missions as compared to the earlier decades, where the teachings on Baptism in the Holy Spirit were consistent and there was a strong emphasis on empowerment for life and service, especially for witness and missions.

AGM reports show that, lately, in the growing business and corporate world, there is also a new area of 'marketplace ministry' led by Christians who have a professional career, business, or corporate vocation, and witness to Christ at their workplaces. This is a current trend in Malaysia, not just in the AGM. Charismatics place more emphasis on lay leadership and making a difference in the marketplace. Churches are also networking and partnering with mission organisations and more church members' participation in missions is through prayer support and missions giving. Thus, the overall importance and need for full-time ministry is gradually decreasing as far as the perceptions of society, including Christian society, are concerned.

There has been a shift from the missionary fervour of the classical Pentecostal approaches, from 'door-to-door evangelism', 'tracting', and 'open air meetings' to contemporary mission approaches of churches organising short-term mission trips for members and evangelism programmes like the 'Alpha Course' for pre-believers, and encouraging more friendship evangelism. A further more interesting change in missional approach is the shift from previously only church planting and evangelism to now also engaging with socioeconomics and integral mission.

The AGM's mission has been moving beyond evangelism and church expansion into social-concern ministry. There are at least 37 organised and registered social-concern works in the AGM, including homes for orphans, dialysis centres, rehabilitation centres, and tuition centres for marginalised communities. These social-concern works are really impacting the community with God's love, the gospel, and a message of hope in this contemporary world.

Bigger churches have continued to plant and support churches and outreaches locally and abroad from the 1990s to the present. From the 1990s there has been a shift in focus to foreign mission trips such as Glad Tiding's mission teams to nine nations, including the

Philippines, Thailand, Cambodia, China, India, and so on. There are churches doing strong mission work during the movement-growth period in the midst of expansion and diversification.

The expansion of missions into new frontiers of social-concern ministries and reaching out to communities is in tandem with the changes in global Pentecostal missions towards expanding their 'social engagement'. This is following the Evangelicals' response to the Lausanne Conference in 1974, and the Lausanne Covenant, which declares proclamation and social service as '"partners" of mission'. The waning eschatological urgency in missions with a new hermeneutical understanding of 'the last days' has prompted Pentecostals to follow the Evangelicals in their missional change to include the 'social dimension', such as 'poverty, social injustice, children at risk, disaster relief and others'.

Sociocultural Factors

As the movement has expanded over time, the small churches planted nationwide have grown in size and also gone through a phase of consolidation. As they have become more financially stable and able to purchase their own church buildings, church leaders have begun to concentrate on church growth and the spiritual maturity of the members, with diversification of ministries and departments.

Many early local pioneers and leaders of the AGM were either first-generation converts to Christianity when they joined in the 1960s, 1970s and 1980s, or came from other Christian denominations. A handful were second-generation Christians. The pioneers who were the youths in the early periods have matured, and now most of them have become grandparents and parents with adult children.

As the AGM grew over the decades, the church grew along with its members. The younger generations were born into families attending AG churches, and at present, many young ministers or members are already second-generation Christians, some with family and children themselves. The surveys and interviews show that the older generation who were Spirit-baptised and filled with the Holy Spirit evangelised and witnessed to Christ (Acts 1:8). However, the younger generations who have grown up in Christian families (not just in the AGM, but across other denominations) feel less urgency or inclination to preach the gospel, share Christ or be a Christian witness.

The younger generation may be more reserved in reaching out, as some may not have had the same impactful experience of the Baptism in the Holy Spirit as the older generation. Many second-generation Pentecostals have not experienced the dramatic conversion experience that their parents had, such as a drastic change of spiritual experience and even persecution from families with staunch non-Christian religious backgrounds. The second generation who grew up in a 'Pentecostal' environment may find the spiritual atmosphere in church a norm and nothing really spectacular or exciting because they have used to it from a young age. Therefore, perhaps the problem among the younger generation is more of being a nominal Pentecostal who has less dynamic experience of the Spirit. Unlike the earlier period, this makeup of the church would impact the discipleship programme of local churches.

This primary focus and purpose of Baptism in the Holy Spirit seen in the older generation is less visible in the contemporary generation. The younger generation feels weird or unfamiliar when it comes to Spirit-baptism and speaking in tongues, and feels spooky about the nature of the Spirit.

The primary concerns of AGM leadership and ministers are for preserving the Pentecostal heritage and passing it on to the next generation. Since 2000, there have been significant remedial steps and efforts to restore Pentecostal heritage, especially among the younger generation. The AGM started a national youth department called Youth Alive Malaysia in 2001 to reach out to youths and raise up youth leaders. Youth Alive Malaysia has started the Youth Enrichment School in 2006 and runs an annual two-week equipping course to introduce young people to theology, ministry, leadership, creativity, and self-development. More than 650 youths have undergone this programme in a decade.

In 2017, Youth Alive Malaysia launched 'iBelieve', which is the 16 Fundamental Truths guidebook and Bible study tool for youths. This marks a beginning of a traditioning and a timely remedial effort to mentor and disciple the young generation in the Pentecostal theology and distinctives. However, this spiritual mentoring will only be effective should all the AGM churches be using this material, not only to teach knowledge about the theology and doctrines, but also to impart the Pentecostal spiritual experiences to their youths, so that they too can experience the presence of Christ in the Baptism in the Holy Spirit and receive the expression of tongues, the gifts of the Spirit, and to hear the Voice of the Spirit in their journey of real faith, missions, ministry, and service.

The style of worship has evolved from hymns to scripture choruses to more contemporary songs. Senior ministers relate that the old Pentecostal songs are more God-centred, about commitment and sacrifice, whereas modern contemporary and Charismatic songs are more 'me'-centred and have shifted from who God is to what He can do for us.

The spiritual atmosphere is not just determined by external influences, but also by internal factors. It is mainly dependent on the personal spiritual convictions of pastors and ministers. The ministers from the pioneering periods seemed to be more resilient, 'die-hard', and served the Lord despite all hardships.

As churches become more established, they send potential church workers for theological training at Bible schools in order to serve in their own churches to meet the growing needs of the local church and members. As such, there is a drastic decline in church planting and mission outreach by ministerial workers compared to the AGM's formative and pioneering period.

Today's generation, with many other priorities and passions, appears to regard full-time Christian ministry as strange and even dispensable. Nowadays, AGM church members are exposed to the more popular response to God's call by professionals and laity serving God in 'marketplace ministry' without the sacred–secular divide. There is a renewed biblical theology of work where God's kingdom, vocation, and calling are undivided as a Christian. Christians do not need to work in the church as a clergy, pastor, or staff, and do not need to be ordained ministers, to be called by God. All Christians in whatever vocation participate in God's kingdom purposes, creation, and providence. This is more of a Protestant understanding and more Christians are subscribing to this trend. There are also the increasing variations of bivocational pastors or tent-making ministries in missions, rather than the old practice of churches sending full-time missionaries to live in a foreign land.

There is an increase in the enrolment of non-full-time students, contrasting with the drastic reduction of the number of full-time students who have a full-time calling as pastors. However, the number of non-full-time students, many of whom are lay leaders, has tripled to more than 700 presently, compared to only 13 full-time students in January 2022.

Modernisation, Technology, and the Digital Age

The emerging culture of technology brings in information on trends from around the world, and from the influence of overseas megachurches, on what it means to be contemporary. Churches need to be careful on how to engage and communicate using technology, ensuring the best ways to bring forth the gospel message.

The internet age has brought about the globalisation and hybridisation of the different streams of Christianity. Church members are exposed to all kinds of teachings and beliefs, so if there is lack of emphasis on the Pentecostal teachings in church, people can be easily influenced by the many other teachings available online. The restrictions imposed due to the Covid-19 pandemic from 2020 to 2021 had forced church services and programmes to be held virtually.

Interdenominational Relationships

The AGM had joined the National Evangelical Christian Fellowship, which was formed in 1982. The BCM later also became a member, in 1989. Since then, there has been an improvement in the acceptance level from mainline churches and the way AGM leaders and pastors relate to other denominations.

The postmodern society generally suffers from boredom, constantly seeking novelty and desiring new things: new technologies, interesting programmes, the latest worship songs, convenience, and feel-good sermons. Postmodern congregations have many other priorities in their private world. Many young and older adults tend to prioritise their careers or vocations above spiritual matters or the church.

Malaysian Social Influences

Along with other faiths in the minority group, Christianity exists with many restrictions governed by federal and state laws, policies, and regulations. The Malays' strong nationalistic fervour and Islamisation has created political, religious, and racial sensitivity in the nation, and limited the way Malaysian churches function in worship, practice, evangelism, and missions.

The global Islamic resurgence and revival has actively taken place in Malaysia since 1970. There has been an erosion of religious freedom, yet Malaysian Christians have been responding and adapting with innovative missional developments: the establishment of seminaries to raise local church leaders and workers, the Bible Society of Malaysia to print Bibles, and an ecumenical formation of a Christian federation among churches in 1985, which has fostered unity among the many denominations and independent churches. Churches and Christian organisations are engaging more in doing good works, charity, and social-concern ministries in the community. At the same time, there has been a growth in prayer movements, mainly among Pentecostal and Charismatic churches, to pray for the many issues of the nation more than ever before.

Modernisation, secularisation, cultural, and societal changes have influenced the present and younger generation with a Western worldview and sceptical mindset. The blending of external theological influences, contemporary worship, and global culture have diluted the conviction in practising Pentecostal distinctives.

The most crucial impact of these contextual factors on the AGM is that Malaysian Pentecostalism is a melting pot of different theological influences and newer teachings, and there is much blending. Overall, these contextual factors are impacting the focus on the centrality of the gospel and Pentecostal identity.

Chapter Five
Stage 3 – Theological Reflections on the AGM's Theological Development as a Malaysian Pentecostal Movement

Introduction

The key to understanding the distinctive nature of Pentecostalism in Malaysia is interpreted in three theoretical explanations: ecumenical diversity, pragmatism, and relevance. Ecumenical diversity being the AGM's interdenominational and international connections, with diverse theological influences impacting the hybridisation of external theological influences within the AGM; pragmatism as the movement seeks means and methods to meet the sociocultural influences in Malaysia; and theological drifts influenced by the Third Wave in the national revival movement.

Theological drifts are widening the tensions. Pentecostalism began as a revival movement and missionary movement, which was how it came to the shores of Malaysia. Over time, revivalism with the focus on Baptism in the Holy Spirit, the gospel, and missions, has changed in emphasis and focus to prayer for revival, united prayer for the nation, and spiritual warfare. In contemporary times, prophecies, dreams, and visions have shifted from the call to missions to a prophetic movement with new national prophecies, new prophetic intercession, enigmatic prophecies, dreams, and visions which cover everything in life, and the popularity of personal prophecies.

AGM pioneers are seeing the infiltration of new theologies, teachings, emphases, and practices in the movement. While Evangelicals have influenced the AGM in solid Christian theology and a strong emphasis on the Word, the Charismatic and Third Wave brought about contemporary worship, emphases on 'power encounter', signs and demonstration of the Holy Spirit, spiritual gifts, 'strategic-level spiritual warfare', 'awakening' the church to transform the nation, and so on. In this process, there has been a broadening in Christian biblical-theological aspects and a widening of the spectrum of pneumatology within the AGM over the decades. To a certain extent, there has been some valid enculturation and responses to the teachings, emphases, and practices of subsequent waves of Spirit renewals as they widely infiltrate global Christianity as the new move of the Holy Spirit. There has been a shift in focus from preaching the gospel and doing good works to 'strategic-level spiritual warfare' for revival in present times.

The external theological influences and practices of Neo-Charismatic Third Wave erode classical Pentecostal core beliefs and distinctiveness. The Third Wave movement bypasses the distinctives of Baptism in the Holy Spirit and glossolalia, but strongly emphasises the spiritual gifts. Third Wavers' claim to being Spirit-filled is theologically different from the classical Pentecostals' distinctive beliefs of Baptism in the Holy Spirit and glossolalia.

The boundaries and distinctions have been blurred and the beliefs and practices blended for many years among Pentecostal, Charismatic, and other Spirit-filled denominations. The crossing over and blending has been more intense over the last three decades, especially from the 1990s to the present, so that it is difficult to differentiate a Pentecostal from a Charismatic or a Third Waver.

These external theologies and practices are shifting the Pentecostal doctrinal emphases and distinctiveness. The Third Wave has a completely different theology and practice from classical Pentecostal, where Baptism in the Holy Spirit and glossolalia are the most distinguishing marks of the AGM. They underplay the importance of tongues and deny initial evidence, as well as glossolalia's direct link to Baptism in the Holy Spirit.

Third Waves' credo and evangelistic strategy of 'power encounter' and 'power evangelism', mainly signs and wonders, and miraculous phenomena, undermine the gospel message with overemphasis on Holy Spirit power. In the majority world, it is often the manifestation of the power of the Holy Spirit in healing, miracles, and deliverance from demonic spirits that accompanies and validates the gospel message. Evangelistic healing rallies are common among Pentecostals and Charismatics and have been effective in winning souls into God's kingdom. The full gospel message must be preached. Hwa Yung asserts, 'For, if our worldviews miss out on some dimension of reality, we will fail to bring the gospel to bear on that aspect of reality. The extent to which we fail to do so, is the extent to which the gospel will fail to be truly liberating.'

S. Chan observes that, over time, classical Pentecostal churches are becoming more Charismatic, forgoing liturgical and biblical norms, and focusing on self and personal experience, resulting in a rapid mutation of Pentecostalism. Third Wave promotes the higher authority of 'apostles' appointed through a council of apostles, with new 'revelations' and reliance on the 'rhema word'. Besides, Charismatic worship has eroded Pentecostals' 'confession of sin, intercession, and testimonies', and shifted to 'praise' with the theology of glory, lacking in trinitarian and soteriological aspects. The issue of prophecy is alarming as it is loosely practised by self-styled prophets and received without question.

The reality of the spirit world in the Malaysian context compels Charismatics, Pentecostals, and Spirit-filled Christians to emphasise spiritual warfare amidst national crises. It would be good for ministers to have dialogues about the diverse theological issues and differences, as the movement seems no longer distinct from other Spirit-filled churches. There is a need to recalibrate and to find a good balance between Christian theology, particularly Pentecostal theology, and the newer teachings, along with the pressing need for revival and transformation of the nation.

Ecumenical Diversity, Pragmatism, and Relevance

The theoretical explanations of ecumenical diversity, pragmatism, and relevance are critical to understanding the theological development of contextualised Pentecostalism. These form the distinctive nature and characteristics of contextualised Pentecostalism in Malaysia.

The Third Wave's focus on 'transforming nations' by their 'Seven Mountain mandate', prophetic prayer, and exercising authorities over nations is influencing Pentecostals and filling the vacuum as the latter shifs focus from end times to the present. These theoretical themes set in as the Pentecostals' waning eschatological fervour shifted its theological motivation in missions from focusing on apocalyptic visions to relevance to society.

Besides ecumenical diversity and pragmatism, seeking relevance has shifted the AGM's emphases and practices mainly to the prayer movement and modernisation.

Relatively, the Third Wave influences are more focused on 'power encounter', spiritual gifts, spiritual warfare, and Christians impacting the arenas of society and nation, but lacking in emphasis on preaching the gospel. The increasing theological tensions and gaps as well as underlying theologies are discussed in the following sections.

Evangelicalism

Evangelicalism in the AG context means accepting training from non-Pentecostal seminaries, using more evangelical scholarship, and putting less emphasis on the Pentecostal distinctives. Evangelicals and Pentecostals share the same core Christian theology, united by the Apostles' Creed and the Holy Spirit, but Pentecostals are different mainly because of their strong emphasis on pneumatology. By late 2000s, ministers trained from non-Pentecostal seminaries, and the crossing over of Christians from non-Pentecostal background to AG churches, became more accepted.

The AGM has gradually mellowed and does not express many Pentecostal values and practices when in public. This is a dilemma: fellowshipping with other denominations is good, but it comes with challenges and requires discernment.

The AGM's increasing exposure to evangelical views provides much good and solid biblical scholarship but lacks emphasis on the Holy Spirit. The use of new delivery methods in the BCM, such as using more evangelical textbooks, and having adjunct faculty who are non-Pentecostals with a strong emphasis on the Word and lacking focus on the Spirit, caused gradual shift in the spiritual atmosphere of AGM churches in the 1990s. The AGM has learned and benefited much from evangelicalism, especially the AG ministers from the 1980s to the present, who are mainly trained using evangelical scholarships.

Too much evangelicalism can dampen the Pentecostal fervour, and in fact Pentecostals have the theology of the Holy Spirit and rich spiritual experiences to offer the evangelical family and ought to be bold in sharing the spiritual dimension of Pentecostal spirituality with the larger body of Christ.

Charismatic

There is a broad distinction between Pentecostals and Charismatics. The distinctiveness of classical Pentecostalism is the gospel, witnessing, and missions, with the spiritual gifts as a demonstration of power to accompany and confirm the gospel. Many Charismatics confine the practice of spiritual gifts to within the church, to ministering to believers and for their spiritual growth, and thus are more ingrown. The Charismatic influence has affected the AGM's Pentecostal distinctives. Chan N.C. observes that there has been lots of cross-hybridisation among the Pentecostals, non-Pentecostals, and Charismatics, so that the lines are no longer distinct.

The dispute on tongues as initial evidence of Baptism in the Holy Spirit has been long debated in biblical scholarship and a topic of contention even since early Pentecostalism. Glossolalia becomes an issue when the AGM has an influx of members from other denominations and Charismatic churches, as well as ministers trained in non-Pentecostal seminaries, as they have different biblical interpretations and convictions. Churches at large which are more seeker-sensitive have cut back on the supernatural and spontaneity of the Spirit. They have become overly concerned about the audience's response rather than believing in the power of the Holy Spirit to work in people's lives.

Charismatics emphasise Baptism in the Holy Spirit and all spiritual gifts – the Pauline sense of *charismata*, signs and wonders, and extraordinary powers, but speaking in tongues – are optional. The Charismatics' strong emphasis on the Holy Spirit brings a balance to the AGM's decreasing emphasis due to the influence of evangelicalism for more than 30 years. There is also the broadening of pneumatological understanding, particularly on the spectrum of spiritual gifts and Pauline teachings on the Holy Spirit, instead of classical Pentecostalism's limited focus on Luke-Acts. Although Baptism in the Holy Spirit as empowerment for missions may not be primary as compared to the AGM's pioneering period, Charismatic churches in Malaysia generally still engage in missions. Perhaps the crossing over between Pentecostals and Charismatics has resulted in mutual influences. But now, both sides are rather similar. I see that there are mutual and valid enculturation and responses, particularly when both are sharing common networks of certain high-profile international guest speakers and conferences.

The Third Wave and Independent Network Charismatic influence has been permeating Charismatic churches in Malaysia, the National Evangelical Christian Fellowship, Prayer United, and the AGM since the

1980s. This has intensified from the 2010s to the present, particularly with the New Apostolic Reformation manifesto, teachings, and practices in prayer movement, prophetic prayer conferences, revival prayer rallies, solemn assemblies, and 'strategic-level spiritual warfare'.

In April 2021, the AG Prayer Commission introduced to the field its partnership with Malaysia United Firewall, with a new website and online platform launched for nationwide, 24/7 prayer initiatives with the theme 'Arise and Build', based on Nehemiah 2:18. This is a united prayer movement in the form of prayer discipleship and partnership of 'prayer altars'. Malaysia United Firewall is playing a coordinating role in establishing unceasing united national prayer and building a 'firewall' of prayer around cities, towns, states, and Malaysia as a whole with its vision from Zechariah 2:4-5, amidst the Covid-19 pandemic and national crises.

Although united prayer movement for the nation did not originate from Pentecostal roots, it has become part of contextualised Malaysian Pentecostalism due to the changes in the sociocultural and religious contexts of Malaysia.

International Relationships

An influential factor for the influx of external theologies of global movements is the close international network of relationships. Inviting prominent international speakers to preach, teach, and conduct conferences and rallies is a cultural practice of AGM and Malaysian megachurches.

The Malaysian context differs much from Korean and Vietnamese contexts in terms of social needs. For the Koreans and Vietnamese, prosperity gospel has been the theology of hope, the 'gospel of need' in their despair and has helped them in upward social mobility. Malaysian Christians have not suffered prolonged war periods, national poverty, and desperation as have the Koreans and Vietnamese. As such, prosperity gospel teachings have been well received and understood differently by the mostly middle-class society in the Malaysian context, which has brought about the focus on blessings, health, wealth, and prosperity. Besides prosperity gospel, Charismatic influences and secularisation also influence social needs. Many churchgoers of this postmodern society have become self-seeking and, as scholars have examined, this is rather universal, which has to a certain extent permeated the Malaysian church landscape as well.

Spiritual Worldview of Malaysia and the Universal Context

Many Malaysian Charismatics, Pentecostals, and Spirit-filled independent churches and believers are drawn to Third Wave's 'strategic-level spiritual warfare' and 'territorial spirits' due to the exposure of their beliefs and experiences of the spirit realm in the multireligious and animistic contexts of Asia and the majority world.

S. Chan highlights that the Asian church exists in the midst of 'ancient family-based religious communities' where the home is the 'primary locus of religious life'. The pervasiveness of animism is seen in the Asian spirit at the grassroots level in the practice of ancestral veneration, prevalent in Asia and Africa. 'In Asia the world of spirits is very much a part of everyday life'. It is possible the Holy Spirit simply replaces benevolent (ancestor) spirits, and the Third Wave teaching best fits this shift. Yeh and Tiénou acknowledge that the spirit world is a reality in majority world theologies, particularly in Asia, Latin America, and Africa, which have strong religious contexts of shamanism, animism, paganism, witchcraft, polytheism, and folk religions. Hwa Yung argues, 'there is also a middle level of "Folk or Low Religion" which consists of beliefs in the local deities, ancestral and other spirits, demons, astrology, and the like who or which act in the world. As this middle level is absent in the Western mind, Western theology has little or no answers for the problems arising here [the Two-Thirds World].'

The adaptability of Pentecostal movements in contextualisation could redeem cultures in responding to primal religious worldviews. Anderson provides the Korean example of the prayer mountain being culturally relevant to Korean religions like shamanism and Buddhism, where belief in good spirits persists, and Christianity, especially in the Old Testament. He expresses, 'There are hundreds of Christian prayer mountains all over the South Korea … Christianity is contextualized by taking the good practices of ancient religions and transforming them with biblical Christian meanings.'

It is quite natural for many Malaysian Christians to accept Pentecostal, Charismatic, and Third Wave teachings on the spirit realm and spiritual warfare, particularly exorcism and 'power encounter'. However, there are exceptions in the many traditional Evangelicals and the modern generation with Western secularised education, where emphases on demonology and the spirit world are less relevant to them.

Prayer Movement

The significant role of the AG Prayer Commission has been more intense especially from 2010 to the present, initiating the prayer movement and 24/7 prayer altars, revival prayer rallies, and solemn assemblies to pray for revival and transformation of the nation.

In the light of Joel 2–Acts 2, the significance of the prayer movement for revival (Joel's prophecy) is the text before the promise of the outpouring of the Spirit. We can see that the foundational Scripture of Joel 2 (Joel's prophecy) is central to the AGM, whether in prayer or in revival, with the new application of repentance prayer before revival, which focuses on earlier verses as a condition of God sending revival to Malaysia. This is a new interpretation and application of Joel 2 in the prayer movement.

In the light of the espoused classical Pentecostal theology and emphasis based on Joel 2–Acts 2, there is a shift in focus of mandates from the Great Commission and full gospel from early AGUSA missionaries (from First Wave) to the new mandate of prayer movement of the Third Wave (and Fourth Wave).

The 'seven mountain' idea started from two similar revelations which Loren Cunningham of Youth With A Mission and Bill Bright of Campus Crusade for Christ believed they received from God in 1975 in slightly different terms: 'seven pillars' and 'seven kingdoms'. It is a strategy to win the nations for Christ with believers influencing the seven critical arenas that shape and transform a nation.

It is vital for Pentecostals to fulfil the Great Commission (Matt. 28:19-20) and bear witness to Christ in every arena of society, to be the 'salt of the earth' and 'light of the world' (Matt. 5:13-16), with the empowerment of the Spirit in Baptism in the Holy Spirit (Acts 1:8, 2).

The difference between the Reformation Manifesto and modern-day missions is that the former emphasises having dominion in every sphere through spiritual warfare and raising the Lord's 'army'. Modern-day missions emphasise practical ministry, social justice, and good works where the gospel is central.

New Theologies, Strategies, and Methodologies of Spiritual Warfare

Third Wave theology believes that the future of the nation belongs to the intercessors, using strategies to pull down evil strongholds. The AGM newsletter reported in 2014, Suubi taught in 'Transformation Prayer Conference' on personal, corporate, and national transformation through restoration of broken prayer altars, namely the 'Personal Altar', 'Family Altar', 'Church Altar', and the 'Territorial Altar', as a 'wake up call to churches to restore their prophetic voice for city transformation, leading to national transformation'.

Third Wave's theology of spiritual warfare is the 'territorial' demonic forces or geographical spirits, taking and transforming the cities and nations through intercession and 'strategic-level spiritual warfare'.

The AGUSA's position on 'spiritual warfare' suggests that there is no solid basis for the teaching of territorial demonic activity. There is no biblical evidence that every city or geographical entity is ruled by a demon. Spiritual warfare is about putting on the full armour of God to stand against the devil's schemes (Eph. 6:11-17). It is incorrect to 'deduce a set formula for encounters with the demonic', meaning ‘strategic-level spiritual warfare’ and prayer strategy are not applicable. However, congregations are to engage in spiritual warfare in corporate intercession, to battle the world at the systemic or structural level, such as government or cultural traditions. The AGUSA believes in praying in the Spirit in spiritual warfare (Rom. 8:26-27; Eph. 6:18; Jude 20).

There are tensions between the Western influences and Asian/Malaysian understandings of the Spirit and spiritual warfare. There is also the tension between the Pentecostals and Charismatics on one side, and mainline evangelical denominations on the other, as regards their different theological understanding and emphases on prayer. The Western worldview is influenced by Enlightenment, philosophy, science, and secularisation, and places less emphasis on the spirit world, compared to Asian worldview. The belief in the demonic realm and ‘territorial spirits’ controlling the natural world is a reality in Malaysia due to the strong animistic influences and primal religiosity. The state of desperation amidst national crises has driven many patriotic Malaysian Christians to engage in spiritual warfare and united prayer for the nation.

All evil powers are subjected to Christ’s authority. Christ’s and the Holy Spirit’s power is above the darkness, above the powers of the world, above the politics, economy, and institutions. In the majority world, Pentecostal movements are highly adaptable to the primal religious worldview. Christians should be aware of two opposite dangers: those not believing in the spirit world and those fixated with it.

Since the 2010s, the AGM leadership has been focusing on the theme of revival, especially at the present time. Most respondents in qualitative research show the desires, prayers, and yearning of AGM ministers and leaders for a spiritual revival in the AGM and Malaysia as a whole.

In contemporary times, the AG Prayer Commission is leading at the frontline to engage 10,000 intercessors and mobilise prayer strategies toward revival and national transformation. The primary focus on 'strategic-level spiritual warfare' to bring revival and transformation of nations is founded on a totally different theology and ethos about revival, eschatology, and prayer as compared to classical Pentecostalism's prayer for missions.

The AG Prayer Commission stresses its prayer initiatives are all geared towards 'revival': to mobilise daily, weekly, and monthly prayers, to establish '24/7 prayer altars', 'build prayer altars' and 'national altars' (spiritual warfare against 'territorial spirits') everywhere because of idolatry defiling the land, to unite Malaysian churches to pray, to conduct 'prayer drives' in towns, cities, and districts to bless the nation, and conduct revival prayer rallies and solemn assemblies (based on Joel 2) focusing on 'revival' and transforming the nation through strategic prayers. The 'mission-centred' element is no longer at the forefront.

In the light of the espoused theology and practice, this seems to be a redirection of focus from the original biblical mandate and commission that Jesus gives his disciples, 'The Great Commission' (Matt. 28:19-20), to the mandate of prayer movement and building a united 'national altar'. This is a vast difference between the AGM's formative period, where gospel was central, and contemporary times, with less emphasis on the gospel due to a diversification of focus. Christians ought to pray and intercede to exercise their faith in God and let his kingdom come on earth as it is in heaven. Christians cannot twist God's arm to send revival using certain strategies or methods of prayer. Being organised in mobilising prayer is good, but the prayer structure and network are not the means to the end. God is sovereign in pouring out his Spirit and bringing revival as He wills, as it is written, 'the wind blows where it wishes' (John 3:8).

New National Prophecies

National prophecies by the Third Wave have been penetrating Malaysian churches and AG in this region. Prophetic intercessors believe they are watchmen that God raises up to take the cities and nations for transformation by spiritual battle, overcoming 'territorial spirits', breaking strongholds, doing prophetic acts, prophetic worship, prophesying, and speaking God's message against the strongholds of cities and nations. Jacobs emphasises that 'the prophetic word is catalytic in bringing changes to societies, cultures and, of course, the Church and nations.'

Although prophetic intercession and spiritual warfare has its place, these should never be above the authority of Scripture and the gospel. The Scripture, gospel, Baptism in the Holy Spirit, missions, and evangelism should remain the central focus in Christianity.

New Enigmatic Prophecies, Dreams, and Visions

The contemporary prophecies, dreams, and visions from the 1980s to present are more enigmatic, as strongly influenced by the Charismatics' and Third Wave's new prophetic movement, particularly 'releasing' of the prophetic word and impressions, 'personal prophecy', 'words of knowledge', and having prophetic conferences. Without the Acts 2 interpretation, the Joel passage itself would not have a strong 'outreach' element but more of a focus on the prophetic unction. The changes in ideas and the nature of prophecies, dreams, and visions practised in the AGM are influenced by the differences in ethos from the First Wave (Pentecostal), Second Wave (Charismatic renewal) to the Third Wave (Neo-Charismatic Movement), from the classical formation period to the present times.

There is a new kind of visioning in the present times compared to the earlier, more literal form of prophecies, dreams, and visions. Some ministers now typically share the visions they receive from God not so much in the form of imagery, but more enigmatically in the form of words, insights, ideas, desires, burdens, inner promptings, and plans. The Third Wave practice of personal prophecies, which cover every aspect of life, has shifted the spiritual atmosphere in many churches as more ministers are exercising their prophetic gifting and people are responding to altar call to be prayed for, and as the Holy Spirit ministers through the 'release' of the prophetic word by the pastor or speaker. This has changed the nature of prophecies, dreams, and visions to be enigmatic and impressionistic as well, and often the need of confirmations, and the increase in body ministry in churches.

Although the nature of prophecies, dreams, and visions changes over time from more vivid imagery to more enigmatic new concepts, the Voice of the Spirit has played a significant role in the growth and development of the AGM from the formative and pioneering period through to the present times.

Wright states that one of the main elements of the Third Wave is to 'equip the saints', empowering all to be used by God: the ‘impartation of spiritual anointing to others through prayer and touch, and the teaching of methodologies for healing.’ ‘The phrase “baptism of the Spirit” was gradually displaced by the more functional and flexible notion of “anointing”.’

The contemporary method of immediacy or instant ‘impartation of anointing’ just by a ‘touch’, especially in big conferences to ‘equip the saints’, has drifted much from the early Pentecostal practice of ‘tarrying’, where the waiting and focus was totally on God. It is not just the length of prayer time per se, but the whole attitude toward God’s presence, Baptism in the Holy Spirit, etc. There is no short cut or quick fix to earnestly seeking and waiting on God, in developing an intimate relationship with Him, and in receiving the Spirit’s empowerment and anointing from God. Indeed, there is the real presence and power of God in the ‘laying on of hands’ and the ‘anointing of oil’, and prayers of healing, anointing, and blessings, which early Pentecostals believed and practised, are biblical practices. In a postmodern society, busy lifestyles and time constraints also weaken the practice of extended hours in worship, prayer, and fasting.

Conclusion

Theologically, the AGM has progressed and developed over six decades with much diversification in the expression of the Christian faith. The AGM has gradually shifted from a revival movement and missionary movement in the earlier decades to having a strong focus on the prayer movement in contemporary times, especially from 2010 to the present. There are both positive contributions and negative elements in these changes.

For the AGM, there has been a valid enculturation, expansion and deepening in the understanding of Christian theology and richer biblical hermeneutics in the embrace of the Evangelical family since the 1980s. Pentecostal fervour has been decreasing over the decades. The pressing need of the AGM and the Malaysian churches in seeking revival and transformation of the nation since the last decade has fostered stronger unity among churches through the prayer movement.

Whilst there are positive contributions and influences among the larger family of Christianity interdenominationally or internationally, there have been theological drifts and tensions in the AGM over time with the influx of new teachings and practices which differ from classical Pentecostalism. This has resulted in a blurring of Pentecostal identity and the boundaries of Pentecostal, Charismatic, and Spirit-filled churches over time. Hence, many participants show concern for the importance of preserving the AGM's Pentecostal heritage and identity in the midst of changes.

Although revivalism and the prayer movement have their crucial place and significance in mobilising prayer and intercession for the nation, these emphases should not overshadow the centrality of the gospel and missions which are Pentecostal distinctives. Pentecostal spirituality has always been about the centrality of Baptism in the Holy Spirit and missiology rather than on prophecy and demonology. Classical Pentecostals engage in exorcism and spiritual warfare (although not on a strategic level), but the main focus is the Great Commission. It is the gospel of Jesus Christ that brings transformation. Through it all, I advocate the upholding of a balanced Christian theology founded upon Scripture and remaining open to the workings of the Holy Spirit as paramount for Christianity.

Chapter Six
Stage 4 – The Way Forward

Introduction

Contemporary Pentecostalism in Malaysia involves the importance of upholding the contemporary Pentecostal spirituality, preserving the Pentecostal identity, enhancing the transformative role of Pentecostal theological education, and progressing in holistic and integral missions. The four domains in the way forward are selected based on the findings in previous chapters and the general decline in classical Pentecostal distinctive practices and fervour.

Contemporary Pentecostal Spirituality: Centrality of Joel 2–Acts 2

Without the outpouring of the Spirit and the centrality of Joel 2–Acts 2, there is no Pentecostalism, and contemporary Pentecostal spirituality is key to Pentecostal living. Firstly, it produces love, zeal, and passion for God and his kingdom, expressed through the preaching of the full gospel and spiritual experiences; secondly, it directs Pentecostal ecclesia, missions, and ministry for the extension of his kingdom. The centrality of Joel 2–Acts 2, Baptism in the Holy Spirit, and glossolalia, and their related key theological themes and practices, are crucial in maintaining a holistic Pentecostal theology and spirituality.

The first way forward in contemporary Pentecostal spirituality is to establish a holistic doctrinal Baptism in the Holy Spirit beyond the limited classical view of Luke-Acts pneumatology. This requires the transformative roles of the Bible colleges and churches in embracing, teaching, and practising the broadened doctrinal distinctives which have been developed by contemporary Pentecostal theologians. The Pentecostal distinctive, particularly the Baptism in the Holy Spirit, is neglected to a certain extent in the life of second-generation Pentecostals.

There is a broader understanding of Baptism in the Holy Spirit, which is the deepening relationship with God. Baptism in the Holy Spirit has to once again be prominent in church services, cell groups, and ministries. The AGM should develop an expanded or revised teaching of Baptism in the Holy Spirit so that the adherents in the wider movement will have a more developed understanding of Baptism in the Holy Spirit and deepen their relationship with God.

Baptism in the Holy Spirit is the 'Crown jewel of Pentecostal distinctives', as it is a theophanic experience of being filled with the presence of the God, a spiritual encounter, and a relationship with the triune God.

Church pastors ought to emphasise on Pentecostal teachings and practice more through church education, discipleship, ministries, and life groups, as well as give room for the Holy Spirit's leading, working, and manifestation in church services, prayer meetings, and small group fellowship.

The second most valuable way forward in Pentecostal spirituality is for glossolalia to be emphasised, theologically understood, and spiritually experienced in order for members to have spiritual conviction in practising it.

Glossolalia is the inaugural sign of the prophetic Spirit. The significance of glossolalia is not just found in classical Pentecostalism, as they claim discontinuity with the larger Christian tradition, but actually both Baptism in the Holy Spirit and glossolalia have roots in the larger Christian spirituality and Christian tradition from centuries earlier. Chan reveals that the Catholic Charismatics find the root of their experiences of Baptism in the Holy Spirit and glossolalia in their own spiritual tradition.

There is a need to develop a coherent theological explanation for this central doctrine of glossolalia, which is lacking in churches today. Bible colleges and church ministers need to teach and advocate that Baptism in the Holy Spirit is a 'theophanic' experience of God's presence, and glossolalia is the Spirit language to communicate with God in His holy presence.

Glossolalia being interconnected with Baptism in the Holy Spirit as 'an experience involving a special kind of relationship with God', and being the distinguishing mark of Pentecostals, it deserves the careful attention of theologians to develop and articulate its theology in a coherent and meaningful manner as it continues to stand as the central doctrine of Pentecostal distinctives, and its spiritual experiences preserved as a central part of Christian life. The AGM's distinguishing doctrinal distinctive is glossolalia.

Spirit-Baptised Church and Believers: A Trinitarian Perspective

AGM's contemporary churches need to pay attention to three key areas: the trinitarian theology, Pentecostal spirituality, and the gospel and missions. AGM churches ought to be intentional in upholding a balanced trinitarian theology in worship and fellowship with the triune God and nurturing the church members in developing a strong Pentecostal spirituality that is rooted in the intimate relationship with the triune God, individually and corporately. One way is to teach the Apostles' Creed to the whole congregation and recite it often so that members truly know and have strong convictions about the core of the trinitarian Christian theology.

Churches also need to be more ecumenical in embracing the wider Christian traditions which are of trinitarian perspectives, and the spiritual liturgy which is core to Christian theology and practice. This is to observe Christian theology more fully throughout the church worship services, in Bible classes, life groups or ministries, and discipleship, while at the same time giving freedom to the Holy Spirit for supernatural works through the ministries of spiritual gifts, healing, miracles, prophecies, dreams, and visions. Some churches may be moving too far away from 'Christian traditions' to the detriment of the congregation, particularly younger generations not being sufficiently grounded in Christian theology. Their relationship with God may lack the trinitarian doctrines and worship, especially when the choices of contemporary worship songs are mostly concerned with self-expression and lack theological content.

Missions and ministries ought to flow out from the relationship with the triune God, be compelled by God's love, and be led by him through the Voice of the Spirit, even without the 'crisis' eschatological fervour or the 'Latter Rain' doctrine, which has waned in the second half of the last century. An intimate relationship with the triune God through Baptism in the Holy Spirit ought to fill the theological gaps of the early classical understanding and motivations.

An essential reminder for the AGM is the 'classic mark of the church' highlighted by Macchia, the Nicene Creed: 'We believe in one, holy, catholic, and apostolic church.' It then goes much deeper to touch ecclesiology.

Although the AGM seeks to preserve its Pentecostal heritage and distinctives or distinguishing marks as a movement, it is only part of a catholic church, as Jesus prayed, 'that they may be one even as we are one' (John 17). The AGM should continue to be united in diversity within the movement, and among the Malaysian churches, and to view all as one body in Christ, belonging to the larger Christian tradition.

Centrality of the Gospel and Missions

The AGM in the classical formative period emphasised the centrality of the gospel and missions, and this is also one of the main distinctives of Pentecostals. The way forward is to re-emphasise the centrality of the Word and Great Commission in the contemporary context.

Ministers need to emphasise the gospel and missions in their preaching and teaching more regularly, as the gospel is the core message of the church and missions are the core practice of the Spirit-baptised congregation. Spreading the gospel and missions is the Great Commission which every church ought to fulfil, and Spirit-baptised believers are empowered by the Holy Spirit to be witnesses to Christ wherever they go (Acts 1:8).

Creating proper platforms like discipleship or mentoring groups in churches for pioneers to share their testimonies on preaching the gospel, evangelism, missions, and the practical steps from the inception of a vision from the Holy Spirit to its fruition, will inspire and instil mission in the hearts of the young generation. They will learn to seek God more, developing sensitivity to the Voice of the Spirit, and be missional in their lives. Inculcating these spiritual experiences through spiritual formation at Bible colleges is key to raising Pentecostal ministers who will disciple their church leaders and members to preaching and living the gospel and being missional in their lives.

True Pentecostal spirituality must be rooted in a deep and strong intimate relationship with the triune God. It is only in the theophanic spiritual experiences of Baptism in the Holy Spirit and a relationship with the triune God that real missional heart, zeal, and passion are ignited and the emphasis on the centrality of gospel and missions is put forth.

A Prophetic Voice in Contemporary Times

Believers need to be the prophetic voice in the nation and community, and to stand up and speak for justice, righteousness, and truth, especially in the public square and marketplace. AGM ministers ought to be sensitive to the Voice of the Spirit to bring God's word of truth and life to the community, and to bring God's love and hope to the world.

Revivalism: Pentecostal Perspective

Revivalism has been the spiritual phenomenon which has ignited missionary fervour and global Pentecostalism since the early 1900s. As Pentecostalism is a revival movement, the AGM also began with an outpouring of the Spirit when revival swept across the country during its formative period, as analysed in Stages 1 and 2. The AGM's historical roots are traced back to the Azusa Street revival, a powerful outpouring of the Spirit which stressed a strong link between Joel 2, Baptism in the Holy Spirit and spiritual gifts being manifested, and there will be more to come until Jesus' return. Today, the AGM believes God continues to pour out his Spirit upon all peoples in different parts of the world and will do so until that Day.

The AGM believes that Pentecostals today are living under the 'latter rain', but one believes that the latter rain is not poured out to the same extent all the time (there were 'lapses'). There are times when the rain almost becomes a drizzle, or just an occasional shower (if I may extend the analogy). So, there is a need to pray for revival, for more 'rain' to come.

Over the last decade in the AGM, the Third Wave revivalist movement has interpreted the revival theme, as directly linked to repentance in the earlier part of Joel's text, in a literal manner. The 'present-day apostles and prophets' have a new interpretation and 'spiritualising biblical events and history' in Joel 2 are a mandate before the promise of revival. The AG Prayer Commission calls for solemn assembly, national repentance, and revival prayer rallies.

God looks at the sincerity of hearts in seeking his kingdom and righteousness for the nations but not at mandates, manifestos, historical models, strategies, methodologies, prophetic prayer conferences, and works of man that bring revival. Revival is the work of the Holy Spirit, not man's ways.

There is continual yearning for revivalism in the AGM, especially among certain senior ministers and leaders, and in the revival focus at the national level, as they recall the pioneering period and see the need for Holy Spirit to revive the movement and the Malaysian church. Revivalist movements and prayer movements are instrumental in mobilising prayers and intercessions, but the main focus should not drift from the Great Commission and Scripture.

Most young people nowadays have not experienced revival before, and few may only hear stories about the revival in the 1960s–70s. In a way, there is a generational gap in terms of spiritual experience, theological understanding, Pentecostal practices, burdens, passions, and expectations. There is also a certain gap between the emphasis on revival rallies at the national level and the autonomy of churches.

Pentecostal Identity

In line with the contemporary Pentecostal Church movement, I strongly propose the way forward for the AGM is in preserving its Pentecostal spirituality, from which flows the new generations of vibrant Pentecostal community, robust Pentecostal ecclesiology, missiology, and ministry in the twenty-first century and beyond. Nurturing the young generations involves inculcating strong Pentecostal conviction and spiritual discipleship through teaching, strong emphases, and practices.

There needs to be a development of the Pentecostal tradition and doctrine in the rediscovery of early Pentecostalism's sacramental and mystical tradition, through retrieval (*ressourcement*) and updating (*aggiornamento*). The discovery of the sacramental and mystical dimension of Pentecostal theology goes back before its Holiness-Keswick traditions to the larger Christian tradition. S. Chan affirms, 'Only as Pentecostal churches begin to revitalize their tradition through *ressourcement* will they be able to preserve their Pentecostal identity. The emphasis on Pentecostal theology as mystical is a helpful step towards articulating a Pentecostal tradition.'

A biblical example of 'true Pentecostal spirituality' is the apostle Paul, the main apostle of vast missionary endeavours who taught Pentecostal spirituality of a Spirit-filled life and church through his letters. It is crucial to pass on to the new generations the emphasis on the whole canonical Scripture and not just classical Pentecostal's favourite focus on Luke-Acts and limited classical views. Pentecostal spirituality should be formed holistically, based on the whole Scripture and the whole counsel of God.

There needs to be the Pentecostal conviction and spiritual discipleship of the holistic Pentecostal spirituality in the trinitarian relationship, the exercising of spiritual gifts, giving room to the Holy Spirit, and focusing on the whole integrated Scripture. It is spiritual discipleship that is able to preserve true Pentecostal spirituality, from which flows Pentecostal living, ecclesia, missions, and ministries.

Pentecostal Theological Education

Pentecostal theological education is far-reaching in raising new generations of Pentecostals, particularly in the theological understanding of a broader framework of the purposes and works of the doctrinal Pentecostal distinctives, which has not been much emphasised in the AGM.

AGM Bible colleges ought to be firm in teaching the Pentecostal identity in order to raise new generations of Pentecostal ministers and leaders for the future. The AGM leadership views that the Bible colleges are responsible for instilling personal conviction in the local pastors and Bible college students or ministers-in-training to teach and emphasise Baptism in the Holy Spirit in the local churches and to build Spirit-filled Pentecostal churches. What is really fundamental is that the Bible colleges need to stay Pentecostal and emphasise Pentecostal ministry and practices, which the church pastors need to preach and demonstrate, and ultimately the churches need to practice, so that they are able to pass on the Pentecostal heritage.

Unity in diversity can be achieved in greater measure through addressing the theological differences of many new teachings of subsequent Spirit renewals. There needs to be an updated Pentecostal theological education to address these unspoken divisions in order for the whole movement to move forward in the same direction. Bridging the theological gap will also enhance unity in diversity among the interdenominational Malaysian Church in united prayer for the nation.

Holistic and Integral Missions

The AGM in its formative and pioneering period has been very strong in missions, and in contemporary times the AGM is still passionate about missions and moving to new frontiers and arenas, and new approaches to preach the gospel.

Churches ought to be contemporary, using the digital platform for missions, and to actively impact the larger community in relating to the government and business sector. They should be involved in the alleviation of poverty in underprivileged communities by mobilising business and social entrepreneurs. Furthermore, they should reach out beyond the socioethnic boundaries to the six million immigrants/migrant workers from various nations, understanding Baptism in the Holy Spirit as the empowerment for missions.

Other new areas of missions are marketplace ministries and nation-building. Thus, in the last two elections in Malaysia, some Pentecostal Christians were involved as lobby groups, pressure groups, and even directly in politics as part of their calling. In the past, Pentecostals would just pray. Hwa Yung urges, 'If the Christian community is to truly live with holiness and with integrity, take a clear stand for compassion, justice and social righteousness, and strive to be agents of reconciliation in the midst of all the ethnic, religious and sociopolitical divisions, they [we] can indeed become God's instrument of transformation for this nation.'

There could be an even wider vision of ecumenism in faith and mission collaborations in the international arena, aiming towards fulfilling the common call of world Christianity, particularly 'The

Edinburgh 2010 Common Call', which emerged from the centenary of the World Missionary Conference.

Conclusion

This chapter serves as a prophecy, dream, and vision for the next generation as it provides suggestions and applications in both theology and mission (practice) to resolve the tensions between holding on to classical Pentecostalism and becoming relevant in the contemporary context in order to move forward. These suggestions provide a balance in the struggle to maintain the AGM's 'DNA' or Pentecostal identity and distinctives in contemporary times.

The outpouring of the Spirit in Joel 2–Acts 2 is the foundation of the Pentecostal movement's theology and practice of Baptism in the Holy Spirit, glossolalia, and spurring the church in missions and service. Baptism in the Holy Spirit being central and the 'crown jewel of Pentecostal distinctives' as Macchia defines it, allows a deepening of intimacy with God and sensitivity to the Holy Spirit. The centrality of Joel 2–Acts 2 and of Baptism in the Holy Spirit enables the AGM to stride forward in the twenty-first century as a contemporary Pentecostal Church movement in the power of the Holy Spirit to preach the gospel, engage in holistic and integral missions, and spread the Pentecostal fires.

Chapter Seven
Summary and Conclusion

This study on the AGM's growth and development from a classical Pentecostal movement to a contemporary Pentecostal Church movement, over six decades from its inception in 1957 to the present, is a piece of original academic research with a unique focus on the AGM in its sociocultural context. It provides a comprehensive understanding of the changes taking place in the perceptible shift from the espoused Pentecostal theology to its contemporary setting.

The most interesting contribution of this study is a holistic and comprehensive pneumatology arising from a conviction that the Voice of the Spirit, mediated by prophecies, dreams, and visions, is an essential spiritual element of the theological, missiological, ecclesiological, and ministerial aspects of the AGM.

Although the Voice of the Spirit is an implicit theology and practice shaped by Joel's prophecy, and the concept of prophecies, dreams, and visions has changed from more vivid to enigmatic imagery these days, it has significant impact on the AGM's growth and development from its inception to the present. Looking into the future, the leadership continues to emphasise the importance of prophecies, dreams, and visions, so that the AGM can be the prophetic voice for the church and nation.

A Contemporary Pentecostal Spirituality for the Twenty-First Century

The research presents the need for a contemporary Pentecostal spirituality for the twenty-first century, resulting from theological interpretation and reflection on the AGM's Pentecostal spirituality as a classical Pentecostal movement and toward a contemporary Pentecostal church movement. The theological factors involve the AGM's blending with evangelicalism, the Charismatic movement, Third Wave, and contemporary influences. The originality of this theological interpretation is a contribution to the movement in understanding the major changes that have taken place over time, particularly in how AGM ministers understand and evaluate both the changes in current theology and practices, and their contextual factors in light of the espoused Pentecostal theology. Due to the hybridisation of these external theologies and influences, many church members, including some ministers, are unaware and have difficulty in differentiating Pentecostals from other, newer movements.

The study proposes a more intentional spiritual discipleship in the preservation of the Pentecostal distinctives, namely Baptism in the Holy Spirit, glossolalia, and missions. This study is vital for the AGM to continue to be the prophetic voice in the movement, in the nation, and beyond. This involves the transformative roles and responsibilities of the leadership, national Bible colleges, church pastors, leaders, and church members as a whole, in rethinking missions, incorporating the advanced contemporary Pentecostal theology in the Bible colleges' programmes and courses, and reinforcing the teaching and practice of Pentecostal distinctives at church level in raising the next generation of Pentecostals.

A Future Direction of Missions for the Next Generation

This study suggests some strategies for the AGM's theological development, transformative practices, and the future direction of its mission for the next generation, in hope to prepare the way for the AGM as a contemporary Pentecostal Church movement to thrive and continue to grow in this century.

There is a need to continually search for new frontiers and adopt new strategies in missions in a multiracial, multicultural, and multireligious country. For example, the demographics are changing with the influx of more than six million foreign migrant workers and refugees over the past decade.

The ultimate goal of this study is that new generations will have a fresh understanding of the centrality of Joel 2–Acts 2 and of Baptism in the Holy Spirit. True Pentecostal spirituality is encountering the living God in the theophanic Spirit baptism and developing a continual intimate relationship with the triune God, from whom flows wholehearted love for God in worship and Spirit-led life, mission, and service, advancing the gospel, and spreading the Pentecostal fires.